PRAISE FOR
— REAL TEENS —

George Barna has taken the guesswork out of understanding today's
teens. And like never before, we now have the means to relate, connect
and communicate the message of hope to this generation.

BO BOSHERS
EXECUTIVE DIRECTOR, STUDENT MINISTRIES
WILLOW CREEK ASSOCIATION

I read everything George Barna writes, and *Real Teens* did not disappoint!
I learned more about this generation of adolescents than from
any other book I have ever read.

JIM BURNS, PH.D.
PRESIDENT, YOUTHBUILDERS

Barna has done it again! He has given the Church an instructive and
informative resource to help us understand today's Mosaic generation.
A book for every parent, youth worker and pastor.

ROGER CROSS
PRESIDENT, YOUTH FOR CHRIST/USA

Barna is in touch with today's teens, and you can be too.
Real Teens is for anyone working in youth ministry. Brilliant!

BARRY LANDIS
EXECUTIVE PRODUCER, "PLUS ONE"

Real Teens gives us a glimpse into the heart and soul of a generation.
Every church must be a hospital for the brokenhearted in this
generation—every Christian an emergency room worker.

RON LUCE
PRESIDENT/CEO, TEEN MANIA/ACQUIRE THE FIRE MINISTRIES

Over the years, I have come to rely on George Barna's thorough and solid research. *Real Teens* is an insightful snapshot of what young people think, feel, want and act upon. A must-read for any pastor or layperson who wants to connect with today's generation of youth.

JOSH MCDOWELL
JOSH MCDOWELL MINISTRY

Real Teens lets us see contemporary youth culture for what it is— a mission field filled with opportunity. Receive valuable and timely advice on how to engage and reach today's emerging generation and understand the changing values and attitudes that lie beneath their behavior.

WALT MUELLER
PRESIDENT, CENTER FOR PARENT/YOUTH UNDERSTANDING
AUTHOR, *UNDERSTANDING TODAY'S YOUTH CULTURE*

If you want to impact our culture and influence the future of our nation, you must examine the lives of teenagers. *Real Teens* is for anyone serious about ministry in the twenty-first century.

STEVE RUSSO
YOUTH EVANGELIST
BEST-SELLING AUTHOR AND HOST OF THE RADIO PROGRAM "REAL ANSWERS"

REAL TEENS

GEORGE BARNA

Regal

A Division of Gospel Light
Ventura, California, U.S.A.

PUBLISHED BY REGAL BOOKS
FROM GOSPEL LIGHT
VENTURA, CALIFORNIA, U.S.A.
PRINTED IN THE U.S.A.

Regal Books is a ministry of Gospel Light, a Christian publisher dedicated to serving the local church. We believe God's vision for Gospel Light is to provide church leaders with biblical, user-friendly materials that will help them evangelize, disciple and minister to children, youth and families.

It is our prayer that this Regal book will help you discover biblical truth for your own life and help you meet the needs of others. May God richly bless you.

For a free catalog of resources from Regal Books/Gospel Light, please call your Christian supplier or contact us at 1-800-4-GOSPEL *or* www.regalbooks.com.

All Scripture quotations are taken from the *Holy Bible, New International Version*®. Copyright © 1973, 1978, 1984 by International Bible Society. Used by permission of Zondervan Publishing House. All rights reserved.

Cover and Internal Design by Rob Williams
Edited by Wil Simon and Rose Decaen

Library of Congress Cataloging-in-Publication Data
Barna, George.
    Real teens/George Barna.
      p. cm.
    Includes bibliographical references.
    ISBN 0-8307-2663-2
      1. Teenagers I. Title
    HQ796.B2784 2001
    305.235—dc21   2001041670

6 7 8 9 10 11 12 13 14 15 16 17 18 / 12 11 10 09 08 07 06 05

Rights for publishing this book in other languages are contracted by Gospel Light Worldwide, the international nonprofit ministry of Gospel Light. Gospel Light Worldwide also provides publishing and technical assistance to international publishers dedicated to producing Sunday School and Vacation Bible School curricula and books in the languages of the world. For additional information, visit www.gospellightworldwide.org; write to Gospel Light Worldwide, P.O. Box 3875, Ventura, CA 93006; or send an e-mail to info@gospellightworldwide.org.

CONTENTS

122 026

ACKNOWLEDGMENTS

This book has been made possible by the sacrificial efforts of many people. Let me mention some of those whose sacrifices went above and beyond the normal call of duty.

At Regal Books, an entire army of people is involved in producing a book. While I don't know each of these literary soldiers personally, I am grateful for their team effort. The warriors with whom I have had the pleasure of working most closely include Kyle Duncan, who has been a warm and encouraging friend through this and many previous books; David Webb, who helped shepherd the manuscript through the in-house publishing maze; Rose Decaen, who was generous in handling my tardy delivery of the manuscript and in clarifying some of the indecipherable footnotes I dumped in her lap; Kim Bangs, who always knew who to ask for help and promptly addressed my idiosyncratic questions; Bill Denzel, who drove the creative process behind the development and marketing of this book; and, of course, Bill Greig III, who has been one of my best friends and most uplifting supporters since we worked on *The Frog in the Kettle* a decade ago. To all of you, and the many who have worked with you behind the scenes, thank you.

I could not have written a book about teens without some keen insights along the way from individuals who work closely with young people day in and day out. While there have been many to whom I am indebted for such wisdom, I'd like to acknowledge two very special people in my life who understand young people so well and helped me to have a clue. Steve Russo is one of the premier youth evangelists in the nation and has been a close friend and ministry colleague for more than a decade. Thanks for your encouragement and the youth intelligence you downloaded. My cousin John Saucier is perhaps the purest, most effective evangelist I've ever known and has taken me with him on days when he does his "gospel thing" among high school and college kids. I am so grateful for your unblemished love for Jesus and your unassailable commitment to reaching young people with the gospel, John. May you stay young and energetic for Christ into your 90s!

The Barna Research Group (BRG) keeps on producing resources for ministries during my writing times despite—or, perhaps, because of—my absence from the office. This is because we have such a stalwart group of ministry-minded team players. I am indebted to the efforts of the 100 or so people who form the company. Special words of thanks are due to Pam Jacob and Carmen Moore, who crunch the data that we turn into useful bits of insight for ministry. Rachel Ables deserves my gratitude for her ongoing leadership. Meg Wells has reduced the burden on me and others by applying her intelligence and command of research and management details to the wealth of projects we undertake. Peter Change and Peter Alvin have relieved all of us of the major headaches related to the technology on which we depend so heavily by focusing on our office network, hardware and software needs and working magic on our website and related needs. Kim Wilson has been a tower of strength, making the Barna Institute, one of the divisions of our company, run smoothly and professionally. Irene Robles and Michelle Niehouse have supported all of us through their willingness to hold all the details together. Jill Kinnaman has handled the brunt of the company's financial and logistical challenges with grace. Cameron Hubiak was an incredible companion and assistant during the year-long seminar tour that took place around the time that I wrote this book, serving with joy and selflessness under often trying circumstances. My wonderful friend and comrade in arms, David Kinnaman, has enabled Barna Research to move beyond survival to growth, handling an incredible volume of details and headaches, while producing high quality work and vision-driven ideas. David has been one of God's wonderful gifts in my life. I thank each and every one of you for the heart, head and hands that you have so consistently and willingly applied to our joint effort to serve the Lord through BRG.

My family, as always, has been incredible. My daughters, Samantha and Corban, sadly but gracefully surrendered their dad to his computer for a couple of weeks to allow this book to come to life. Their joy and love have made focusing on this book more difficult but also more significant as they approach their teenage years. My wife, Nancy, has once again sacrificed more of her life and best interests than anyone should ever have to, in order to help me and contribute to the development of God's kingdom through this book and the ministry of Barna Research. Nancy has been an amazing supporter of mine for almost three decades, abandoning many of her own heartfelt desires, to support and invest in the vision that God implanted in my mind and heart nearly 20 years ago. My greatest worry for her is that when she gets to heaven she will not be able to lift her head because of the numerous jewels in her crown, awarded for her incredible servanthood. I am a man blessed with the support of friends, coworkers and family who make it possible to serve God with energy and single-mindedness.

None of this would be worth anything if it had not been for the model of love and grace provided by Jesus Christ. He is my Savior, my friend, my guide, my Lord and my mentor. He has called me to serve Him in a special and wonderful way, for which I am grateful. May this meager work of my hands find some utility in His hands.

Introduction

This is a book about the changing of the guard in American culture. This transition takes place every 15 to 20 years or so. In this case, I am talking about the ascendance of a new generation—one that is replacing the much misunderstood and oft-maligned Baby Busters. The new guard is the Mosaics. Maybe you've never heard that name before. Get used to it. They will revolutionize your world.

My advice is that you forget everything you've read about generations with initials (e.g., Gen X, Gen Y, Gen Z) or those described by the new century (e.g., the Millennials). Journalists typically fabricate the analyses of these groups by using a handful of personal stories and anecdotes, as if those tales represented an entire generation's experience. Everyone loves a good story, and anecdotes can make dry sociological analyses come to life. But there remains a very significant difference between objective, scientifically derived data that provide a panoramic, replicable view of a population and the subjective, hit-or-miss pop analyses served up by reporters searching for a hook that will meet a deadline. Even a cursory examination of how magazines, newspapers and TV newscasts treat generations shows that they typically define a generation as a group that covers a 5- to 10-year span. That in itself is a problem: a generation cannot be 5 to 10 years in breadth; the traditional span is approximately 15 to 20 years.

In this book I will describe the findings from our recent nationwide surveys among teenagers to present a broad analysis and interpretation of their current state and likely future. There will be a special emphasis upon the group that will reshape our culture most dramatically in the coming decade—the Mosaics.

The Mosaics are the youngest of the five generations that coexist within America today. Those generations are the Seniors (born in 1926 or earlier); the Builders (1927-1945); the Baby Boomers (1946-1964); the Baby Busters (1965-1983); and the Mosaics (1984-2002). The oldest of the Mosaics have been around for more than a decade and a half, but it is not until a group reaches the age of 12 or so that social scientists and marketers start to pay serious attention to them—and have a sufficient body of credible information upon which to draw conclusions about the group. We are finally at the stage where we can begin to project the nature of the Mosaics.

OUT WITH THE OLD

For the past 15 years, whether they acknowledged it or not, the Baby Busters were busy changing our world. They had the unenviable task of supplanting the Baby Boomers in order to experience their own "15 minutes of fame." That task was made all the more difficult—and less desirable—by the fact that Boomers do not like to be upstaged by anyone. As the showdown approached, and aware that imitation is the sincerest form of flattery, Boomers quickly noticed that Busters were not paying their respects. In fact, not only were Busters failing to mimic Boomer tastes, lifestyles, ideologies and priorities, but they were also brash enough to noisily trash Boomers and repudiate virtually everything for which they stood.

If there was ever a group that should have understood the need to enter the cultural scene with a major statement, it should have been the Boomers. After all, they had replaced the Builder generation in the '60s with a series of high-profile, in-your-face transitions. Elvis Presley and Chuck Berry, the most radical musical pioneers adored by the last of the Builder teens, were positively angelic in comparison to the wild hair, daring lyrics and ear-shattering rock of the Beatles, Jimi Hendrix, The Who and Led Zeppelin. *Ozzie and Harriet* and *Leave It to Beaver* faded in the wake of adventurous telecasts such as *Saturday Night Live* and *Soul Train*. Woodstock, the cultural coming-out party of Boomers, was unlike anything the Builders had ever imagined, much less carried out. Rather than accepting conditions as they were, Boomers questioned everything—until they got the answer they wanted. Instead of prolonged dating experiences, Boomers championed cohabitation; when that didn't work, they readily embraced divorce as a costless solution to difficult and irritating relationships. Alcohol, the demon drug of their parents' and grandparents' generations, lost its prominence as drugs like marijuana, heroin and cocaine took center stage. While the Builders had devoted themselves to fostering a nation of prosperity and civility, Boomers sought to gain control of the decision-making apparatus from day one, intent upon redefining authority, burying tradition and increasing their profile in business and government. The arrival of the Boomers signaled the end of predictability, the rule of fairness and the notion of the common good.

It would be a gross mistake to suggest, therefore, that the uppity ways of the Busters were a novelty. In many ways, teens in the '80s and early '90s were simply following in the unfortunate footsteps of their predecessors, pulling out all the stops to be declared victorious in the game of Cultural Emergence. The Boomers had introduced a new notion into our culture: complete and unapologetic disregard and disrespect for the prevailing cultural norms. Boomers had a single goal: to win on their own terms. It should have been no surprise, then, that their successors had absorbed the lessons and principles that made Boomers the most studied, feared, appreciated, loathed and successful generation in America's history.

The relationship between the Builders and Boomers has been known as the Generation Gap. The interaction between Boomers and Busters might best be characterized as the Generational Cold War. Relations between the two groups remain frosty to this day.

In fact, the Boomer-Buster script reads like a definition of "polar opposites." Boomers were the last of the modernists; Busters were the initial postmodernists. Boomers were the ultimate capitalists; Busters took pride in their sloppy work habits, their disinterest in careers and their refusal to become educated simply to make a better living. Boomers believed in the entrepreneurial way of life, but the irony is that the most successful Boomer entrepreneurs were those who cashed in on the technological breakthroughs developed by the Busters.

Under the long-term management of Boomers, rock music lost its edge. That edge was picked up by the two musical styles that are the legacy of the Busters: rap and grunge, which are genres that ooze with anger, sarcasm, independence and dissonance. Boomers took pride in making "business casual" the norm; Busters took it a step (or two) further. In fact, the most daring of Boomers had sported shaggy hair, unkempt beards and bandanas. Busters smirked at such temporary displays of disrespect, opting instead for permanent signs of cultural contempt and self-determination through tattoos and body piercing.

If the street motto of Boomers was "Get ahead or get even," the theme of Busters was "Get lost and get a life." Boomers sought unbridled sexual pleasure, engaging in serial marriages and record-breaking numbers of extramarital trysts; Busters avoided marriage as a show of disdain for the emotional abandonment they had experienced as the products of those millions of broken relationships. After a brief flirtation with Eastern religions, Boomers surprisingly accepted Christianity as their faith of choice (although without much depth of commitment). Busters finished the job the Boomers had only started, ushering in an era of low-key, New Age spirituality that has affected every component of American society.

AND IN WITH THE NEW

So here we are, experiencing the entry of the newest generation's teen-agers, just as unprepared for their antics and demands as we were when the Boomers and Busters nudged their way to national prominence. As Boomers turn to plastic surgeons, miracle medicines and postmodern philosophy to deny their age, and Busters continue to whine that they have never received their due and thus refuse to relinquish the recent attention that their technological expertise has afforded them, the Mosaics are struggling to claw their way onto the main stage of cultural significance. What will they bring to the party? I feel confident suggesting that there are three "guarantees" we can make regarding the Mosaics.

First, they will be the most numerous generation in America's history. The Baby Boomers gained their name because they were the first generation that had 4 million or more live births in a single year. They were 76 million strong by the end of their run in 1964. (They have since expanded to some 80 million, thanks to immigration.) The Baby Busters, so named because they were not as numerous as the Boomers, were actually the second-largest generation in American history, comprised of 68 million individuals by the end of 1983. (Immigration has inflated their numbers to about 76 million today.) Population experts are projecting that the Mosaics will weigh in around 76 million by the end of 2002. By the time immigration adds to their numbers, they will easily exceed the record-setting Boomers by several million people. Along with their massive size will come other "mosts": they will likely be the longest living, the best educated, the wealthiest and the most wired/ wireless.

Second, they will likely baffle millions of people with their unpredictable, quixotic, seemingly inconsistent and idiosyncratic values, beliefs, attitudes and behaviors. Boomers left little to the imagination as to where they stood regarding war, sexuality, church, materialism and other issues of the day. Busters were less overt and communicative but no less definitive. Whenever there was any doubt as to where the Busters stood, it was a pretty safe bet that you could simply identify the Boomer perspective and assign the antithetical view to Busters.

Mosaics, however, are an unusual amalgam of perspectives, blending the ideas and behaviors of Boomers and Busters with their own unique views and ideas.

Third, Mosaics will provide the Church with a massive and fertile population for evangelism and discipleship. However, the outreach strategies utilized to penetrate the Boomer and Buster populations will be doomed to failure if applied to Mosaics. Our research clearly demonstrates that Mosaics will be the least churched generation of the past century unless Christians modify the approaches they use to influence the faith development of this spiritually open and spiritually savvy segment.

NAMING THE GENERATION

I clearly recall a conversation with an intelligent, well-informed ministry colleague when I first described the Mosaics. "Hey, wait a minute. What did you call them? Where'd you get that name? I thought they were called the Millennials, or Gen Y or something like that. Mosaics? What's that about?" He couldn't get past the name. Perhaps that's your first stumbling block, too. Let me explain why I think the name fits the emerging generation snuggly.

We could adopt a name like "Gen Y" (chosen by the media because this group follows the Busters, whom they often named "Gen X"—journalists are extremely proficient with the alphabet). However, young people hate being labeled by single initials. At least the robots in the Star Wars series had multiple letters and numbers—R2D2 or C3PO. Busters hated the "Gen X" label because it suggested that they were not even worthy of a name (thus raising the abandonment issue again); it insinuated that they are a generic group (might as well have been "brand X", they figured); and it conveyed a lack of personality on their part.

But generation naming is becoming tougher than you might imagine. Boomers accepted the "Baby Boom" title because it was true, they were the first generation to be named in such a high-profile way, and the name implied their strength in numbers. It has been all downhill since then. The

Busters, true to form, have yet to like any name associated with their tribe. They dismissed the "Baby Bust" label because it irrevocably tied them to the Boomers—a group they despised and did not want to be associated with. "Postmoderns": too heady. "MTV Generation": too one-dimensional. "Thirteenth Gen": meaningless to anyone other than historians, and even then it intimates that their existence is defined by that of 12 preceding generations. To my knowledge, no one has ever conjured a name that satisfies the Busters, Xers, MTVers, Postmoderns, 13th Gen'ers or whatever you want to call them. (With apologies to the sensitivities of that group, I will henceforth refer to them as Busters, for ease of identification.)

While not as picky, the Mosaics have voiced their displeasure at the brand names offered to them. "Gen Y" is a cop-out. They find "Millennials" disturbing, because it suggests that their defining characteristic is that they happened to be born around the turn of the century. It's a very sterile name. We have not researched it yet, but I bet they'll reject "Mosaics," too.

If the term "Mosaics" received fair consideration, though, young people would discover that it solves many of these identity problems while communicating significant substance about them. It is a term that is multifaceted, as well. This group of people is "mosaic" because

- their lifestyles are an eclectic combination of traditional and alternative activities;
- they are the first generation among whom a majority will exhibit a nonlinear style of thinking—a mosaic, connect-the-dots-however-you-choose approach;
- their relationships are much more racially integrated and fluid than any we have seen in U.S. history;
- their core values are the result of a cut-and-paste mosaic of feelings, facts, principles, experiences and lessons;
- their primary information and connection—the Internet—is the most bizarre, inclusive and ever-changing pastiche of information ever relied upon by humankind;
- the central spiritual tenets that provide substance to their faith are a customized blend of multiple-faith views and religious practices.

Put this all together and the result is a mosaic in various dimensions of life. You could probably make a strong argument that the Boomers would have been better named "Rebels" or "Iconoclasts." The Busters now might be best characterized as "Tribalists" or even "Invisibles." I'd bet money on the fact that 30 years from now the name "Mosaics" will still be a comfortable fit for this new generation.

WHY TEENS MATTER

Studying teenagers is a task undertaken by few Americans. For the most part, parents hope to survive the teenaged years of their kids so they will feel they have earned retirement; teachers expect icon status for managing young adults; and church youth workers see such a ministry as a means of retaining a "hip" or "in touch" image among their peers and elders. The tactics employed by the individuals who interact with teens tend to be hand-me-down routines rather than creative, thoroughly researched strategies. Now that I have mentioned this, it may even be dawning on you that it's not worth your time to read an entire book about teenagers!

Let me challenge you to continue reading. I think there are at least four very significant reasons why every adult should take the time and make the effort to understand the teenaged bastion that populates our country.

- Teenagers largely define the values and leisure endeavors of our nation.
- Our economy is substantially shaped by their choices as consumers and by their work habits in the labor force.
- The nature of the family, the foundational unit of our society, depends on how teenagers prioritize family and approach parenting.
- The future of the Church will be determined by their faith contours and commitments.

In other words, the substance of our culture hangs in the balance with the changing of the guard every couple of decades. Why? Because once people hit their mid-20s and beyond, they are who they are, and the degree of personal change they undergo in terms of character and values is minimal. If the content of our culture—manners, traditions, language, leisure pursuits, values, customs and beliefs—is going to change, the transitions will be championed by those who have the fewest routines and the least to lose through change, and who possess the greatest freedom to experiment with life's fundamentals.

Of all the different age-defined populations, high school and college students feel most capable of taking audacious risks in virtually every dimension of their lives. They rarely feel encumbered by the tyranny of personal history and remain unconscious of societal limitations. Once people accept massive doses of responsibility—such as jobs, housing payments, car ownership, marriage, parenting, community service, health care—the stability, consistency and weight of daily personal choices lessens their adventurousness and freedom to experiment. Teenagers, in particular, walk the fine line between ample information, intelligence and experience versus responsibility, commitments and expectations.

THE INFORMATION SOURCE

Most of the information that people receive regarding teenagers is from stories in the media. Those stories are often based upon unusual events or behaviors that have come to the attention of a journalist, who then uses a handful of anecdotes as the basis for some sweeping conclusions. Because those reports rely upon a small number of people from the same geographic area who are not representative of the larger population from which they are drawn, and do not use a consistent means of information gathering and processing, the results are interesting stories that may not provide accurate insight into reality. In most cases the information is intriguing but neither objective nor representative.

The insights provided in this book are founded on a very different base of information: random-sample surveys with teenagers from across the nation. As part of our ongoing tracking of the values, attitudes, beliefs and behaviors of teenagers, the Barna Research Group conducted five surveys among teens during the past two years. Because each survey used a nationally representative random sample of teenagers, we are able to project the results of those studies to the aggregate population of American teens. In total, the views of more than 3,000 young people are included in this analysis. If you would like more details about the research methodology we employed, there is a description in appendix A of this book.

BUCKLE YOUR SEAT BELTS

Understanding teenagers provides you with a vital link between the past, the present and the future. If you hope to not only comprehend where our culture is going but to also have some influence or say in that movement, then you must examine the lives of teens.

Join me on a guided tour of the amazing, alarming, alluring world of America's teenagers. In the pages that follow, we will explore their attitudes, image, values, relationships, hopes and dreams, lifestyles, politics, beliefs and religious practices. You will receive a bird's-eye view of the Mosaics, and be among the first on your block to have a clue as to where these young adults are taking our culture and how it will affect you. Toward the end of our journey I will challenge parents, churches and teenagers themselves to reflect upon some of the major decisions and opportunities they will face in the coming few years. Prepare yourself for a ride that can compete with the best roller coasters our theme parks have to offer—and with a final destination that is much less predictable.

LIFESTYLES AND INFLUENCES

Those of us who use scientific methods, such as surveys and statistical analysis, to interpret reality have a tendency to create tools to help people understand the results of those methods and thereby comprehend what is taking place around us. Sometimes those tools consist of new terms we coin; other times the tools are unique ways of perceiving conditions. For instance, the notion of a generation is such a contrivance. There really is no such thing as a generation: It is an idea used to identify a group of people who have a common place in time and have consequently experienced similar influences and opportunities that have shaped their development. Another tool we have created is the idea of a life stage, which is a passage that people go through at predictable ages or periods in their lives.

Indisputably, teenagers see themselves and their world differently than do people of other age groups. Some of the observable attitudinal and behavioral differences are attributable to the natural maturation process that occurs during various life stages, while other differences are related to generational distinctions.

For instance, feeling physically attractive is a *life-stage* reality: It is something that is influenced by one's physical development, which is generally beyond the control of the teenager. Thus, younger teens are dealing with growth spurts, hormones and other body changes that cause all kinds of identity crises and self-doubt emanating solely from their physical appearance. In the same way, older teens are likely to register greater stress than young teens because of the multiplicity of new and significant pressures they experience. They must simultaneously handle physical maturation, dating and peer acceptance, sexual opportunities, post-high school educational and occupational uncertainties, after-school job responsibilities, driving and related expenses, academic performance pressures, civic duties, moral and ethical challenges, and so forth. Like everything else in life, being a teenager is a series of trade-offs. One might enjoy the freedom and independence that the teen years bring but wilt under the multitude of pressures that come with those freedoms and opportunities.

Over the past several years, we have had the chance to speak with several thousand teens across the nation regarding how they look at themselves, their world and their future. Clearly, there are some perspectives that are related to their age and life stage.

- The younger they are, the less likely they are to say they are physically attractive.
- The younger they are, the less likely they are to claim to be emotionally sensitive.
- The older they are, the more likely they are to feel stressed out.
- The older they are, the more likely they are to become politically aware and the more likely they are to have more precise ideological positions on social and political issues.
- The older they are, the more likely they are to be searching for meaning and purpose in life.

In contrast to these life-stage concerns, a current *generational* distinctive relates to attitude. While the older teens still cling to the Buster-driven tendency to see the glass as half empty, the younger teens reflect the Mosaic penchant for describing the same glass as half full. Busters tend to see themselves as the victims of a society that does not understand them and that largely ignored them until their technology skills became marketable—that is, until they could be used by others for selfish gain. Mosaics have a deeper sense of innate self-worth, largely based upon the generational perspective that life will be very good for them and that society does care about who they are and how they mature.

There are some clear generational attitudes that emerged from our research among teens. Here are a few of the transitional patterns we have observed thus far. Compared to Busters, Mosaics tend to

- be more upbeat—they are less cynical, less skeptical and less pessimistic;
- be more interested in developing a meaningful career and doing what must be achieved to facilitate a viable career;
- view education as an irreplaceable preparation for life, rather than as a means of proving their worthiness and gaining acceptance from their parents;
- consider religion, spirituality and faith to be a positive dimension of life, but neither central nor critical for fulfillment;
- utilize a mosaic thinking style;
- exhibit less emotional sensitivity—they take a joke, handle criticism and understand the context of abandonment more readily;
- feel more vitally connected to other people and to their culture.

Keep in mind that none of these comparisons makes one group right and the other wrong, or means that one group is better than the other. These kinds of insights merely help us understand how to relate to each group more appropriately and how to see the world through their eyes.

BLURRED AROUND THE EDGES

In many cases you may not see much difference between 15- and 16-year olds, who are technically from the Mosaic generation, and kids who are 17 and 18 years old, who represent the tail end of the Buster cohort. This is to be expected for several reasons. First, remember that this notion of generations is a tool created by social scientists to help track and interpret social change. No one can definitively say when one generation starts and another stops: It's all determined by the analyst whose work you are exploring.

Second, a generation describes a shared experience of cultural change. Before the incredible transformations that irrevocably altered the world in the twentieth century—radio and television broadcasting, airplane travel, desktop computing, the Internet, DNA, genome research, nuclear energy—cultural change occurred much more slowly than it does these days. Perhaps there was a substantial redesign of cultural foundations—language, traditions, values, relationships, icons, symbols and so forth—every 60 to 80 years. For a while, it appeared that such cultural change had sped up to generate a new cultural context every 20 years or so. In that social setting, following generations made a lot of sense. Today, however, our society experiences fundamental, extensive and rapid changes that effectively reinvent America's culture every five years or so.

Consequently, it is not surprising to find that there is much blurring around the edges of what we traditionally describe as a generation. You will find many of the youngest Boomers acting and thinking more like Busters who are 10 years their junior. You will find many of the oldest Busters who are more like Boomers than their own peers. The same fuzziness occurs between Busters and Mosaics: There are not rigid cutoffs that prevent the oldest Mosaics from continuing the Buster lifestyle and mind-set or the youngest Busters from perceiving and behaving more like Mosaics.

There are many examples of the blurred-edges phenomenon between Busters and Mosaics. Both groups appear to be highly relational; love being bombarded with mass-media images and information;

have short attention spans; value the nuclear family; want a comfortable existence without having to "sell out" their values to achieve it; are comfortable with regular change; have integrated digital technology into the foundation of their operational existence; and are comfortable with contradictions.

The important thing to keep in mind is that all of the generational descriptions and prescriptions are useful for one purpose: to help us understand, serve and love each other better. The value of identifying or identifying with a generation is not that we can label or stereotype people, but that we can see them more easily for who they are and know how they got there, where they may be headed and how we can serve and relate to them more appropriately. At this stage we have only the "early returns" on the Mosaics. They will continue to evolve as they shape their cultural reality and it continues to shape them. Given the pace of cultural change, we may even discover that what would have traditionally been deemed the Mosaic generation—that is, a 20-year segment of people—is best understood by being divided into two or three smaller aggregations, each with its own set of unique attributes.

THE DAILY ROUTINE

In years gone by, we spoke of the daily routine—the predictable activities and adventures that could be charted well in advance with a high degree of certainty. For today's young people, routine is the enemy: They love the hectic, unpredictable, ever-changing, fast pace of their existence. When things seem to get slow or predictable, they deem life too boring and meaningless. To most young people, a life that lacks surprises and discontinuity seems to be no life at all.

But there are two key elements that teenagers feel must be incorporated into their experience. The first of those is relationships; the other is mass-media experience. Take away relationships and you steal the heart of their world; remove the mass media and you eliminate their sense of connection with the larger world and the drama they love to be exposed to through a sense of shared culture.

Relationally, teenagers strive to have a serious connection with both family and friends every day. Most of them succeed. In a typical day, 96 percent of teens will spend some free time with friends. How interesting—and revealing—it is to discover that they are more likely to have a meaningful conversation with their friends during a typical day than they are to have such interaction with either their mother (70 percent do so) or their father (53 percent). (It is worth noting at this point that two out of three teens—67 percent—also say that they pray to God in a typical day.)

Notice, then, that teens are more likely to consult friends than parents (or siblings) regarding things of importance to them. Notice that teens are perhaps more likely to seek God's help or direction with challenges than they are to seek such advice from parents. Notice that teens are more likely to have significant interaction with their mom than with their dad. But also notice that a majority of teenagers indicate that they have meaningful dialogue with their parents during a typical day. Parent/teen conversation is not completely absent. We discovered that millions of parents agonize over their desire to have even deeper, more meaningful involvement in the lives of their maturing young people, but at least many teens recognize their parents as trusted or accessible advisors.

MEDIA EXPERIENCE

The influence of the mass media upon the minds and hearts of America's youth cannot be overestimated. Teens spend an average of four to six hours per day interacting with the mass media in various forms. For instance, we discovered that 94 percent listen to the radio, 91 percent play audiocassettes or compact discs, 89 percent watch television 69 percent read a magazine, 58 percent read part of a book in a typical day and 52 percent use the Internet. In addition, 79 percent use a computer during a typical day (in many cases involving exposure to content on the Internet), and most teens use the telephone for additional communication. Cumulatively, this represents an enormous amount of external input and stimulus every single day. It also helps explain why researchers contend that the typical American is exposed to more than 2000 commercial messages every day.

Perhaps the most underestimated influence on the lives of teens is their music. Journalist John Weir studied the appeal of "electronica" music among teenagers, a sound created by morphing sampled sound bites into new, beat-heavy, dance-oriented music. He concluded that, "every generation needs a private language that people over 30 can't translate."[1]

Our research confirms that music may be the single, most important cultural creation of a generation, a special form of communication that is theirs forever, even if it is borrowed or mimicked by others. Boomers will never give up their guitar-based rock. Busters will retain strains of rap and hip-hop until they die. Mosaics will carve out their own sound, probably morphing their current preference (bubblegum pop from boy bands and pop princesses) to a new rock derivative sound that will be their own special blend of past influences and personal flair. The sounds emanating from Backstreet Boys, 'N Sync, Hanson, Britney Spears, Christina Aguilera and other stars of the moment are setting the stage for the new language, symbolism and icons of the emerging generation.

For teenagers, music is much more than mere entertainment or a diversion from the stress of homework, household chores and worries about the future. For millions of young people, music produces a life philosophy for them to consider and follow; cultural heroes and role models to look up to and imitate; values and lifestyles to embrace; a common language to employ that sets them apart and provides a distinctive identity; and the opportunity to develop community related to a shared sense of common sound, ideas or artists.

Teen musical preferences change on a regular basis. Industry insiders recognize that the tastes of teens fuel the music industry, so understanding their preferences is of critical importance. The recording industry, radio stations, television networks, advertising agencies and movie studios all have deeply vested interests in understanding, responding to and shaping the musical preferences of teenagers and college students. Unfortunately, while many in the entertainment industry view the development of pop stars and cultural icons as mere business, the values and views proposed by those societal heroes influence the lives of millions of people—especially the lives of the most impressionable individuals, our young people. The platform accessed by entertainers can result in very positive outcomes, if the platform is used responsibly—or in harmful outcomes, if the platform is used irresponsibly.

MUSICAL PREFERENCES

Currently, the favorite styles of music among teenagers provide insight into the values they are embracing as reasonable and appropriate. In fact, the first insight we glean is that their tastes change remarkably quickly. In past decades, a recording artist who scored a hit might remain popular for five years or more. Today, given the short attentions spans of Americans, the plethora of new artists, the emphasis upon having many options from which to choose, the absence of a sense of loyalty, and the importance of music as a self-defining resource, it is unusual for an artist to remain on top for more than a year or two—perhaps for the duration of that one hit recording.

In 1997, our interviews with teens showed that their favorite genres were alternative rock (listed by 27 percent as their favorite musical genre), rap/hip-hop (22 percent) and R&B (10 percent). No other genres were named by at least 1 out of 10 teenagers. Other styles that were mentioned by at least 3 percent included hard rock (6 percent), country (5 percent), classic rock (5 percent), soft rock (4 percent), contemporary Christian (4 percent) and gospel (3 percent).

By 2000, the list had undergone some radical changes. Alternative rock dropped out of favor and was replaced by traditional rock. Rap/hip-hop maintained its core following and actually became the most popular sound among teens. R&B retained its level of favor, while pop jumped into the upper tier of genres. Christian music experienced a slight dip in popularity.

THE MUSICAL LIKES AND DISLIKES OF TEENAGERS

Style of Music	Favorite Style	Dislike It
rap/hip-hop	25%	20%
rock	22	12
R&B	13	2
pop	11	8
country	6	33
Christian	3	1
dance/techno	2	1
classical	2	3
Latin	1	1
jazz	1	2

In fact, some styles have a stronger "anti-following"—that is, a contingent of kids who dislike the sound—than they have adherents. Country leads the pack in this regard. Although country music is the fifth most popular genre among teens (6 percent claim it as their favorite, and others enjoy it), it is also the most widely disliked style (listed by 33 percent). Rap/hip hop, while retaining its top dog position among the favorite genres, also emerged as the second most widely disliked style (20 percent). Even venerable rock music has a sizeable audience of detractors (12 percent, plus another 3 percent who singled out heavy metal as a style they disdain).

Similar patterns were evident in terms of the music purchased by teens. This is no small matter, since teenagers spend literally hundreds of millions of dollars every year on recorded music. While sales of alternative rock and contemporary Christian declined, rap/hip-hop stayed on top, followed by rock and pop recordings. Country fared quite well in the number of units sold to young people.

There were some noteworthy subgroup differences regarding musical preferences.

Boys were more likely than girls to identify rock and rap as their favorite styles, while girls were more likely to choose either pop or R&B as the type of music they prefer. Boys were more likely than girls to purchase hard rock. Girls were more likely to buy soft rock and country.

Pop and rock topped the charts among whites but were largely ignored by blacks. Similarly, most of the country music purchased by teens was among whites.

Blacks were twice as likely as whites to select rap as their favorite category (although rap was the second-ranked genre among whites). A huge majority of black teenagers—about four out of every five—had purchased rap recordings in the past year. R&B ran a close second to rap among blacks but barely charted among whites. Purchase patterns showed that few blacks bought hard rock or alternative rock, both of which were mainstays among whites.

Breaking from earlier patterns, Hispanics have shifted their attention away from rock and have widely embraced rap. They were much less likely than other teens to purchase hard rock or country recordings.

A larger percentage of blacks than either whites or Hispanics had purchased any contemporary Christian music (CCM) in the past year. CCM also counted large numbers of teens living in the South, with its most fervent fans being those who were politically conservative, most active in church life and had accepted Christ as their Savior. There were significant differences in preferences according to geographic region. CCM has a significant presence in the South but has a very slim following in the Northeast. Pop found its biggest base in the Midwest, with the South close behind, but had a limited following along the coasts.

Older teens were more likely than their younger counterparts to like dance/techno and country. The youngest teens were the dominant fans of pop but were less excited about R&B and country—perhaps because of each genre's emphasis upon intimate relationships.

The data indicate that born-again[2] teenagers have musical tastes similar to those of their non-Christian peers. The only real difference in stylistic preferences was that born-again teens were substantially more likely to list contemporary Christian (CCM) as their favorite. Even among the born-again group, however, just 1 out of every 14 (7 percent) identified CCM as his or her preferred style.

Of special intrigue is the fact that 1 out of every 3 teens who purchased CCM in the past year was not born again. That represents significant growth in purchases by non-born-again teens in the past three years—at the same time that CCM purchases among born-again teens have declined. (Overall, about 1 out of every 10 non-Christian teens and one-third of Christian teens bought a Christian recording in the past year.) In raw numbers, that means more than 1 million teenagers who are not born again bought at least one CCM recording within the past year. Also of interest is the finding that about half of all born-again teens purchased some rap or hip-hop recordings within the past year.

Of related interest is the fact that most teenagers' parents have no idea what music their kids listen to or the lyrical content of their musical diet. Given the importance of music in shaping the values and ideals of our young people, we would be well advised to devote greater attention to this dimension of our youths' development.

It is also worthy of note that few Christian artists have risen to the level of enduring role model or hero among teens. DC Talk, the rap-turned-rock ensemble, may be the closest thing that today's Christian teens have to a reigning pop idol—and even this star is losing some of its luster in terms of popularity. Once again, the changing nature of the culture and music can be seen. For a long time, Christian artists such as Amy Grant and Michael W. Smith were seen by millions as the epitome of the clean-cut, wholesome followers of Christ whose music and lifestyles were worthy of closer examination. For better or worse, kids these days are hard-pressed to identify such icons. Given the constricted nature of stardom these days, even mega-selling artists like Kirk Franklin and Jars of Clay may well be forgotten by the time you finish reading this book!

THE REIGN OF TECHNOLOGY

Technology has always fascinated and attracted Americans—especially young Americans. Whether the invention was the radio, automobile, television, jet travel, cable broadcasting, digital watches, VCRs, cell phones, personal computers or the Internet, we have consistently been drawn to advances in technology that possessed the potential to significantly affect our lives. For young people, the adoption of new electronic devices has provided them with a novel means of communication, a "cutting edge" image and has helped to define the youthful lifestyle.

Americans spend massive amounts of time and money on technology. Currently, American households contain an estimated 1.6 billion consumer electronic products at a cost of more than $407 billion. The average household spent in excess of $1,000 buying new technology in the form of computer and electronic hardware and software—and that level of spending is unlikely to diminish in the near future.[3] If teenagers have anything to say about it, that level will accelerate rapidly.

The Internet has certainly been the focus of technological innovation during the past few years. In a short period of time, the Internet changed from being a little-known means of communication developed and utilized by the military to a global communications and information network that shrank the world into a global village and created an entirely new culture. At the start of the '90s, less than 2 percent of American adults used the Internet, and less than 3 percent of all businesses had a Net presence. At that time it was a tool used primarily by the upscale audience and geeks.

At the start of 2001, 57 percent of the adult population made use of the Internet, either at home, at work or at play. The Internet has already transitioned from being an esoteric appliance that is irregularly used to a tool that is relied upon for a variety of purposes by most people.

If analysts are taken aback by the rapid growth of Internet usage among adults, that incidence pales in comparison to the proportion of teenagers who use the Net—currently some 91 percent! Teenagers also go online more frequently than do adults, and tend to stay online for longer periods of time. If the Net is just becoming a comfortable addendum to the adult media world, it has already become an indispensable focal point of the teenagers' world of communications. It is relied upon for self-expression, information and entertainment.

FREQUENCY OF INTERNET USE

	Teens	Adults
every day	41%	30%
several times a week	27	15
once a week	10	4
2 to 3 times a month	8	5
once a month	3	2
less than once a month	2	1
never	9	43

The chances of Internet use continuing to climb are virtually guaranteed. New applications are making the Net increasingly "necessary" in people's lives and in business settings.

Like adults, teenagers use the Internet for a wide variety of activities. As the accompanying table shows, the most universal value of the Internet is as a source of information. More than 9 out of 10 adults and teenagers acknowledged using the Net for that purpose. Adults and teens had roughly the same incidence of using the Net for maintaining existing relationships, too: 47 percent of adults and 42 percent of teens indicated that the Internet has been helpful in this regard.

A COMPARISON OF HOW ADULTS AND TEENAGERS USE THE INTERNET

	Teens	Adults
find information	93%	96%
maintain existing relationships	42	47
buy products	29	47
check out new music/videos	64	35
play video games	38	24
participate in chat rooms	46	18
make new friends	35	13
spiritual or religious experience	12	8

Usage patterns varied considerably in regard to other applications. Adults were much more likely to use the Internet for buying products (47 percent versus 29 percent of teens). That proved to be the only application that was noticeably more common among adults than young people. Teenagers were more likely to use the Net to explore new music and videos (64 percent among teens, making this the second-highest application tested, compared to 35 percent among adults); to play video games (38 percent versus 24 percent, respectively); to participate in chat rooms (46 percent versus 18 percent, respectively); and to make new friends (35 percent versus 13 percent).

The remaining application evaluated was usage of the Internet for religious or spiritual experiences. Adults and teenagers had similar incidence levels—8 percent and 12 percent, respectively—and this application rated eighth among the eight possibilities explored.

The ways in which teenagers use the Internet are also instructive. The older the teenager becomes, the more likely he or she is to use the Internet for gathering information. The youngest teens are more likely to use the Net for developing new friendships and for religious purposes. Teenaged girls are more likely than boys to maintain existing friendships electronically, while boys are more likely than girls to play video games and buy products digitally. While whites are more likely than nonwhites to keep up friendships and seek religious experiences via the Net, blacks are more likely to check out new videos and music.

Of particular interest amid the data is the profile of young people who use the Internet for religious involvement. Not only do the youngest teens and whites seem more attracted to the Net for spirituality, but also those who are born again and who are more spiritually active than the norm use the Internet for religious purposes. The most intriguing connection is that Net-based religion appeals more to rural kids than to those who live in the suburbs and urban areas. It may well be that since most rural churches are small in numbers and have fewer flamboyant services and programs, the Internet levels the playing field for teens who live in more remote areas.

The ways in which teens are using the Internet continue to evolve even as the medium itself is evolving. First, keep in mind that the Net has transitioned from a widely used technology to a universal life form among teens: in 1997, about two-thirds of all teens used the Internet, with about half doing so on a daily basis. By the beginning of 2001, more than 9 out of 10 teens had used the Net with some regularity, including 4 out of 10 who went online daily.

HOW TEENAGERS' USE OF THE INTERNET IS CHANGING

Application	1998	2000	Change
find information	93%	93%	—
check out new music/videos	56	64	+14%
participate in chat rooms	51	46	-10%
maintain existing relationships	28	42	+50%
play video games	33	38	+15%
make new friends	34	35	+ 3%
buy products	7	29	+314%
spiritual or religious experiences	4	12	+200%
sample size	*620*	*605*	

Second, realize that over the past three years we found that the uses of the Net that grew most rapidly were for buying products (the incidence of which rose by 314 percent among teenagers) and having religious or spiritual experiences (which increased by 200 percent). Using the Net to maintain existing relationships also grew by 50 percent. Meanwhile, the Net lost ground as a place to facilitate conversations: chat room use dropped by 10 percent. Using the Net for information remained a universal application, while there was evidence of minor growth in its use as a place to preview new videos and music (+14 percent), as a source of games (+15 percent) and as a means of making new friends (+3 percent).

THE CHURCH AND THE INTERNET

There has been considerable debate and controversy regarding the potential of people to abandon the physical church—that is, the bricks-and-mortar congregational entity—in favor of a "virtual" church experience, or engagement in the "cyberchurch." Our research underscores the fact that a substantial movement of people away from the physical church to the digital faith arena is likely to take root in the coming decade. Busters and Mosaics will be at the forefront of that movement.

Very few teenagers (2 percent) currently rely upon the Internet for their entire faith journey or even as a supplement to a physical-church experience (7 percent). Relatively few expect to do so in the near future. However, their expectations regarding reliance on the Internet for faith purposes is telling.

When we asked people directly about their likelihood of using the Net for religious purposes, there was a clear sense of uncertainty—and openness—regarding the possibility. When asked to predict whether they will use the Internet for at least part of their religious experience five years from now, relatively few teens said they would definitely do so (1 percent) while a significant portion (one-fifth) said they would probably do so. This is interesting if for no other reason than that the "will definitely do so" percentage is substantially lower than the current percentage of teens who are already doing so today.

While these figures seem straightforward—and, to some extent, appear to suggest that the cyberchurch will never get off the ground—approaching the issue from a different angle provided a completely different perspective. The numbers escalated substantially when, instead of asking about macro-level use of the Net for faith, we queried people about their potential use of the Internet for a variety of specific faith-related purposes.[4]

Among teenagers who said they were open to the possibility of using the Internet for spiritual purposes five years down the line—a group that constitutes 3 out of every 5 teens—huge proportions of young people admitted a leaning toward incorporating the Net into their faith practices. The most popular spiritual uses of the Internet would be reading devotional passages online, submitting prayer requests and listening to archived religious teaching online—all three activities deemed likely uses of the Internet by at least half of this teen subpopulation. Nearly half said they would participate in a chat room or discussion group regarding faith, while 4 out of 10 teens said they expect to participate in independent study courses on faith matters and to buy books or study guides about religion or faith. More than one out of every three plans to buy religious music online; to participate in a real-time, online Bible study; and to be mentored in spiritual development by a "virtual coach." Even the least appealing alternative of the options posed—a real-time, video-streamed worship experience—was something that one out of every five teens said they would take advantage of in the future.

Why, then, are the figures lower when we ask if they plan to rely upon the Internet to supplement or even replace the physical church in their faith journey? To a large extent, it is still psychologically jarring for many youths to admit that they are disassociating from a social institution that is so ingrained in the fabric of our culture. They have a tougher time admitting to themselves that they are apt to leave the physical church than they are to take overt steps toward doing so. In fact, we learned that many young people do not even think of their faith-based explorations and experiences on the Internet as church related.

HOW TEENAGERS EXPECT TO USE THE INTERNET FOR FAITH IN THE FUTURE

	Teens
read a short religious reading to motivate, challenge or focus	55%
submit prayer requests to a group that prays for people's needs	54
listen to religious teaching from online archives	50
participate in a chat room or discussion group regarding faith	46
participate in independent study course on faith matters	40
buy books or study guides about religion or faith	39
buy religious music	37
participate in a Bible study online, in real time	36
be mentored/coached in spiritual development	36
participate in an online class that meets regularly	29
worship through real-time video streaming experience	21
sample size	*374**

Note: * based upon all respondents except those who said they will "definitely not rely upon the Internet for at least a part of your religious experience within the next five years or so."

The high levels of comfort expressed with these different forms of online faith experience are both inescapable and highly significant. The message is clear: The physical church, as we have always known it, is about to be altered in fundamental ways by the emergence of the cyber-church. Whether or not you deem this transition appropriate is not the relevant question: The change is in process and is unlikely to be halted unless the Internet itself experiences a permanent crash. The pertinent questions relate to what you are doing to facilitate an appropriate and responsible use of the Internet for bringing people into a proper relationship with Christ and His people.

By the way, here is an observation about these findings that may give you some direction in your reflections about the future Church and how we might best prepare to provide youth with a valid digital faith experience and journey. The response pattern shown in the accompanying table indicates that people are least interested in the most intense possibilities. Notice, for instance, that the lowest-rated faith applications were worship, coaching, a class and a Bible study—arguably the endeavors that demand the most intense involvement. The experiences that registered the most positive reaction were the least personal or safest options: buying resources, asking for prayer, reading passages and listening to taped sermons, and independent study. In this sense, the cyberchurch suffers from the same difficulties as the physical church: People want value but at minimal personal investment.

Undoubtedly one of the key challenges we face as we dive headfirst into this age of technological achievement relates to control. Do those who use the new technologies control its use, or does the application of the technology eventually enable it to take over our lives and dictate who we are and how we behave? Technology and technological tools, whether they are innovations for ministry or weapons of mass destruction, have no ethics—only the creators and users of the technology do. This means that we bring our ethics into each circumstance. With a few exceptions, every new tool can be used for good or for evil purposes; as the developers and implementers of the technological advances, we shape the ultimate value of the tool.

Regarding the Internet, we must remember that it is primarily an information and communications conduit. It is people who choose the quantity, quality and substance of the information that gets channeled through the web of electronic connections. Without some prevailing cultural consensus about moral truth and ethical parameters, the Internet will be a no-holds-barred frontier in which ministries compete against other organizations and causes amidst a forest of appropriate and inappropriate offerings. How can we, as the Church, shape the Internet for the purposes of the Church, exploiting the positive Kingdom possibilities represented by the Internet, without compromising who we are, what we stand for and how we serve others?

The rise of a cyberfaith culture and population must cause us to renew a commitment to truth and morality in all that we do. The apparent inevitability of people gradually moving toward greater exploration and development of their faith with the assistance of digital technology raises more questions than it answers—and certainly raises more questions than any individual feels capable of, or inclined to answer. But we must address these very real and advancing issues.

TEEN LIFESTYLE ELEMENTS

Just as the life of adults is defined by busyness and variety, so is the life of our nation's teenagers. In a typical weekday, 9 out of 10 teens will do homework. Earlier we noted that media use is prolific, while relational activities—both among family and friends—are also part of their daily regimen. Prayer is a daily exercise for most teens. Less common exploits include reading from the Bible (35 percent do so during a typical week) and keeping a personal diary (22 percent make an entry at least weekly). Drinking wine, beer or other alcoholic beverages—illegal for all of the individuals interviewed—takes place at least once a month among one out of every four teens (24 percent).

As a highly interactive group, teens have a high regard for conversation. The topics of conversation vary, but our surveys indicate that about 4 out of every 10 teens spend some time during a typical day conversing with friends and family about religious matters (43 percent said they do so). A similar proportion (41 percent) focuses on political matters.

The religious activity of teens is substantial, although it does not necessarily occur as regularly as many adults might think. The most common religious activities are praying to God (67 percent say they do so within a typical day) and reading their horoscope (52 percent). Prolific but less frequent activities include reading from the Bible (35 percent) and discussing religious matters with friends and family (43 percent). Even less regularly, teens are likely to engage in meditation (12 percent do so within a month), consult a medium or spiritual advisor other than a Christian minister (10 percent), chant (9 percent), fast for religious reasons (9 percent) or do yoga (4 percent).

One observation to distill from these statistics is that the teenaged life is a diverse life, with every day filled with a variety of activities and interactions. The survey also points out that if a teen is inclined to engage in any one of these activities, he or she will probably do so on a regular basis. For instance, the number of kids who read a book in a typical day and within a three-month period is virtually identical. Similarly, the number of kids who spend time on the Internet varies little on a daily basis compared to a quarterly basis. The greatest distinctions appear to relate to religious activity. For example, many teens who do not read the Bible or pray or discuss religious matters on a daily basis may still engage in such activity on a less regular timetable.

Attention has been drawn to the ethical and moral perspectives and behaviors of young people. Given their tendency to reject all moral absolutes, it would not be surprising to find that their behavior reflects an "anything goes" mentality. Fortunately, if this self-report from teens is credible, the translation of relativism to every walk of life has not yet become pervasive. The survey found that within a typical three-month period it was common for teens to engage in at least one at-risk behavior. Those activities ranged from drinking alcohol or smoking cigarettes to cheating on a test, exam or some other type of evaluation (20 percent); looking at a pornographic magazine or movie (14 percent); having sex (14 percent); using an illegal, non-prescription drug (10 percent); and stealing money or some other material item (5 percent). These behaviors do occur, but at infrequent intervals.

SUBCULTURES WITHIN TEEN AMERICA

Throughout this book I will reference the value that teens place on belonging to their "tribe"—i.e., their closest circle of friends that is, in many ways, a surrogate or at least supplementary family unit. Sometimes it is easier to understand the importance of a young person's tribe by seeing that aggregation as people who represent a unique subculture. I believe there are at least 20 different teenage subcultures existing in the United States today. Teenagers often belong to multiple subcultures—sometimes because they are transitioning from one to another, sometimes because they have multiple interests that require variety in their tribal loyalties, sometimes because they are searching for their place in the larger culture.

Here are a few of the more common subcultures, most of which probably exist in your vicinity. The names undoubtedly vary from locale to locale, and in some regions of the country these particular labels may be viewed as offensive—my advice is that you focus on understanding these subcultures and embrace the name that the youths in your area choose for themselves.

- *Boarders*: kids whose relationships and free time hinge on skateboarding, rollerblading or surfing.
- *Gothics*: fascinated by gothic clothing, makeup, music and environments. Among their trademarks are black clothing, silver jewelry, pale skin and candles.
- *Gays*: homosexuals who have proudly emerged from "the closet."
- *Skinheads*: hyper-conservatives who have racist leanings, freely use physical intimidation and support violent means to advance their reign.
- *Greenies*: climbers, bicyclists and hikers who love the outdoors and support environmental causes and animal-rights groups.
- *Geeks*: a.k.a. nerds or "digit-heads," these are the computer whizzes of their age group, and they spend hours engaged in learning computer programming, surfing the Internet and tinkering with electronic gadgetry.
- *Jocks*: the physically fit youths who live for competitive sports.

- *Rappers*: often black and Hispanic youths, these are kids who love rap and hip-hop music, have a distaste for authority and see violence as a means to an end.
- *Metalheads*: covered with tattoos and body piercing, this group is characterized by motorcycles, loud heavy metal music and clothing that is peppered with silver studs and chains.
- *Preps*: a.k.a. "buttondowns," they are focused on academics and getting into the premier colleges, saving money and becoming successful in their chosen career.
- *Jesus Freaks*: these youths are known to pray at school, carry their Bibles with them, attend youth-group meetings during the week and wear jewelry and clothing that proclaim their faith in Christ.
- *Gearheads*: the new form of "greasers," these folks live for their cars, working on their engines and waxing their vehicles to a shining reflection.

Personal identity has always been a major concern of teenagers. The last two decades have introduced a much wider variety of choices available to young people. The age-old tradition of developing habits, symbols and nuances that distinguish one's group remains in force. What we see on high school campuses across the nation are clans (i.e., subgroups) comprised of member tribes (i.e., affinity households). Just as greasers and jocks used to battle each other for turf and respect in the '60s, today's subculture war games are generally harmless efforts by youths to define themselves and to set themselves apart as belonging to a community of like-minded peers. Tattoos and body piercing, hallmarks of several subcultures, are simply the new symbols of identity, independence and core values. Clothing styles are not about fashion but community, since the styles one wears associate them with a given subculture.

EXPERIENCES RULE

Consider all that we have just revealed about the daily experiences and perspectives of young people. The result of this review of teen reality is that we begin to realize that while family, friendships and personal achievement are important, experiences are what rule their lives. In a fast-paced, relativistic, information-drenched culture, with fluid relationships and ever-changing faith views, the constant that keeps life meaningful and invigorating is the latest and most satisfying experience. Events, adventures and unexpected encounters make each day a new and satisfying episode in their unfolding story. That which does not provide a fresh experience is deemed to be of lesser or no value.

This drive for experiential reality is altering everything in America. Pines and Gilmore, among others, have noted that to build a following and have influence in our culture today, one must develop memorable and personally engaging events or experiences.[5] It is the event that attracts attention, creates value and satisfies the individual's longing for more than the mundane routine of life. Teenagers, raised in the fast-paced world of videos and the interactive, personalized and boundaryless world of the Internet, are leading this foray.

There is a key implication in this for those who wish to make the faith journey a core element of the lives of teens. Looking at that journey through the lens of experience-driven reality raises questions about how we make their spiritual path one of creative, inspiring, rewarding and challenging opportunities to grow. Young people recognize that they are in a life stage that demands personal change and definition. They are willing to undergo the difficulties associated with personal maturation—as long as the quality of the journey holds the promise of justifying the depth of the challenges. They want to enjoy the journey. To enjoy it, they want pleasant, revealing and surprising experiences. They will resist rote, predictable exercises in favor of that which makes the effort extraordinary. Those who wish to see true spiritual and personal transformation occur in the lives of young people cannot afford to ignore the implications of the experience-driven lifestyle.

Like so much that we face in our culture today, you may not feel comfortable with that mind-set or like that approach to spiritual development. My advice is simple and not meant to be sarcastic: Get over it. You don't have to like how they learn or what they demand in order to grow—you just have to deal with it. They live in an experience-based

world and crave unique and fun experiences. The Christian faith ought
to be capable of delivering transformation—the ultimate experience—in
a context of creativity and exuberance. We may all be better off for the
effort to do so.

Notes

1. John Weir, "Hot Sound," *Rolling Stone* (August 1997), p. 54.
2. In all of our research and throughout this book, the term "born again" is based on
   asking people's response to two survey questions. In the first question we ask people
   "Have you ever made a personal commitment to Jesus Christ that is still important
   in your life today?" If they answer yes, we then pose the second question, which
   relates to what they believe will happen to them after they die. One of the seven
   options we offer is "After I die, I know I will go to heaven because I have confessed
   my sins and have accepted Jesus Christ as my Savior." We then classify people who
   provide that answer as born-again Christians. We do not ask people if they consider
   themselves to be born again. We also do not truly know who is born again—only God
   does—but we use this process of estimation to give us a sense of what is happening
   spiritually among those who rely on God's grace rather than works or universalism
   for their salvation.
3. These figures are from the Consumer Electronics Manufacturers Association, as reported in *Research Alert Yearbook 2000* (New York: EPM Communications, 2000), p. 29.
4. The source of this data is YouthPoll, conducted November 2000 by the Barna
   Research Group, Ventura, CA.
5. Several books have been written about this phenomenon. Among the best are B. Joseph
   Pines and James Gilmore, *The Experience Economy* (Boston: Harvard Business School
   Press, 1999); and Michael Wolf, *The Entertainment Economy* (New York: Times Books,
   1999).

CHAPTER 2

WHAT THEY'RE THINKING AND FEELING

Various psychological tests strive to measure two key emphases in people's lives: how they think and what they feel. In fact, one prominent diagnostic classifies everyone as either a "thinker" or a "feeler." Yet each of us thinks and feels to differing degrees. Understanding the dynamics of what teenagers think and feel will give us even greater insight into who they really are and where they're headed.

THE NEW TEEN PROFILE

For those who feel more comfortable with people who are upbeat, focused, stable and accepting of traditional behaviors, the emergence of the Mosaics will be a welcome change from the quixotic, often-pessimistic Busters. In fact, as we study the two generations, it becomes clear that we are not just in a period of transition from one generation to another, based on chronology; but perhaps we are also witnessing a fundamental and lasting shift in attitudes and perspectives.

For instance, notice the decidedly upbeat perspective most teens possess. Four out of five say they are optimistic about their future. A smaller proportion, but a majority nevertheless, says they have high hopes for the nation's future. The prevalence of skepticism, a hallmark of the Busters, is waning. As we enter into the post-Clinton, post-dot-com era with economic storm clouds on the horizon, this enthusiasm may be tempered somewhat; but the basic attitude of these young Mosaics seems to be more firmly positive than what has been evident for the past decade.

Indeed, some of this optimism has less to do with their environment and more to do with the positive view that teens have of themselves. Three out of four consider themselves to be physically attractive. Almost as many believe that other people see them as leaders. A majority claims to be very popular. These are not the views of a dour, downcast group with little hope for the future.

The emotional state of America's teens also explains the positive thoughts they harbor about both the present and future. More than 9 out of 10 teenagers describe themselves as "happy." Four out of 5 say they are trusting of other people. Only one-third describe themselves as "stressed out" (although the proportion depends on which segment of teens you talk to). Since Mosaics are a well-connected group, it is not surprising to discover that only 1 out of every 10 considers himself or herself to be lonely.

To really understand teens, though, we must look beyond their sense of hope. Growing up in a high-tech, information-drenched, mobile society has enabled these kids to mature in some dimensions of life well beyond what their age would merit. Notice, for instance, how many young adults have taken on the persona of self-reliance: Almost 9 out of 10 revel in their self-sufficiency (whether real or imagined) and independence. A similar proportion deem themselves to be responsible individuals. All of this, of course, is supported by their sense of being savvy: 4 out of 5 claim to be "very intelligent." In short, they are comfortable with who they are. Most teenagers are confident that they can handle whatever the world may throw at them, and they are anxious to make a positive difference in a world that, despite their optimism, they believe needs substantial change.

In comparing these teens with their counterparts of a decade earlier, the differences are staggering. As we entered the '90s, teenagers were less sanguine about their future, less self-confident and more likely to see virtue in isolating themselves, as a generation, against the tyranny of the Boomer hordes who were economically, emotionally and environmentally ravaging the world. The music that they turned to—"grunge" (a.k.a. alternative rock), along with the hostility expressed in much of the "gangsta rap" that prevailed—reflected the cynicism, disappointment and profound sense of abandonment felt by millions of teenagers.

That same angst is not present among current teens—at least not in relation to Boomers and all that they do and stand for. The despair that teens embrace is based upon the obstacles to their ascendancy in society. As we will discuss in subsequent chapters, the goals and expectations of the new millennium teens reflect their interest in getting ahead. They insist on doing so on their own terms, of course, but they uphold the importance of making a place for themselves in the same society that their older brothers and sisters had, just a few years earlier, written off as not worthy of such effort.

SELF-IMAGE DISTINCTIVES

As you might expect, though, you cannot lump all teens into one group and assume that you have captured the nature of them all. The teen world is an amalgam of splinter groups, sometimes differentiated by demographics, sometimes defined by attitudes and behaviors, sometimes best described by faith elements.

An example of the distinctions within teen America relates to gender. Upon comparing the self-perceptions of male and female teens, we discovered that there was a significant gender gap related to 11 of the 19 self-evaluation items used in our research. In general, the differences suggest that girls are more likely than boys to be optimistic, reflective, insecure, religiously oriented and self-confident. The only dimension on which boys surpassed girls was in viewing themselves as very popular.

Similarly, there were differences in self-perception based upon ethnicity. White teenagers were more likely than nonwhite teens to say they are trusting of other people and to admit to being stressed out. Nonwhite teens were more likely than their white counterparts to say they are skeptical, searching for meaning in life and see themselves as very intelligent, physically attractive and very popular. Interestingly, nonwhite teens were also more likely to portray themselves as both religious and spiritual. However, there was no difference in terms of being described as a committed Christian: 6 out of 10 teenagers, regardless of their racial heritage, claimed that attribute.

Teenagers who are born-again Christians were somewhat more likely than non-born-again-Christians to claim they are very popular, trusting of other people and very intelligent. Not surprisingly, they were also much more likely to describe themselves as religious, as spiritual and as committed Christians.

HOW TEENAGERS VIEW THEMSELVES
(N=620)

Attitudes/ Perceptions	All	Age Group			Caucasian?		Born Again?			
		13-14	15-16	17-18	Male	Female	Yes	No	Yes	No
optimistic about the future	82%	79%	82%	84%	78%	86%	83%	80%	84%	80%
searching for meaning in life	56	55	52	64	50	64	53	62	55	57
optimistic about America's future	56	57	54	58	52	60	57	54	57	55
skeptical	45	41	47	49	44	46	43	49	44	46

	All	Age Group			Caucasian?		Born Again?			
		13-14	15-16	17-18	Male	Female	Yes	No	Yes	No
Public Image										
physically attractive	74	65	74	85	74	74	69	85	77	72
seen by other people as leader	69	68	67	71	67	70	68	70	72	68
very popular	57	59	51	63	61	52	52	66	64	54
Faith Related										
religious	64	64	61	70	61	68	61	73	89	52
a committed Christian	60	64	62	53	56	66	59	63	91	45
spiritual	60	60	61	60	54	67	56	68	85	47
Emotional/Relational										
happy	92	92	93	93	92	93	94	90	95	91
trusting of other people	80	88	82	68	81	80	84	73	84	78
emotionally sensitive	55	44	55	68	46	65	55	54	56	54
stressed out	36	26	40	46	29	45	40	29	30	40
lonely	11	8	10	15	10	11	10	13	10	11
Behavioral/Personal Qualities										
responsible	91	90	90	96	88	95	90	93	92	91
self-reliant	86	81	88	90	86	86	85	87	87	85
very intelligent	79	75	77	85	76	82	75	87	86	75
Political										
mostly conservative	15	10	15	20	16	13	16	14	22	12
mostly liberal	13	7	12	18	12	13	12	12	10	14
somewhere in between	67	74	65	61	66	67	66	69	61	68

Note that even among the non-born-again teens, half said they are committed Christians, half called themselves spiritual, and half claimed to be religious. Part of the culture of American teenagers is to engage in religious thought, speech and activity. Further, as we find among adults in America, many teens assume that their religiosity qualifies them as Christians, although they do not have any type of ongoing relationship with Jesus Christ or do not base their understanding of salvation upon their confession of sins and acceptance of Christ as their Savior.

BEHAVIORAL STYLES

A different spin on teenage identity is derived by assessing their behavioral styles. Using a behavioral profile we developed, which examines the unique ways in which people think, feel and behave, we gained some valuable insights into the teenaged population. These insights should help us to enable teens to see themselves more accurately and to help us engage with them and help them to mature more appropriately.[1] In our recent surveys with teenagers, we discovered that to the largest proportion of teens, relationships matter, but to most teens details and getting things exactly right are less important than the general flow of events. Here's a thumbnail sketch of what our testing revealed.

Nearly half of all teenagers (45 percent) are described by the Influencing style (*I*). These are "people people." They tend to be animated and lively individuals, and they live for interaction with others. These are compassionate people who like to help others whenever possible. Typically upbeat, they are free thinkers and have a tendency to solve problems by talking them through out loud. Often warm and charming—they crave popularity—they struggle to balance their natural spontaneity and their tendency toward superficiality.

Influencers are high-strung and can be overly sensitive. Their emotions sometimes color their decision making, producing bad judgment and unfortunate choices. While they do not always use the best judgment when making decisions, they have the capacity to motivate others to get involved by the sheer force of their energy and enthusiasm. They respond well to personal encouragement and approval, and they live in fear of losing their influence over others. To minister most effectively to *I*'s, help them become more intentionally analytical and organized. Teach them how to base their decision making on facts rather than snap judgments and to rely upon analysis rather than democratic rule.

One out of every four teenagers (27 percent) is characterized by the Dominance style (*D*). These are your classic type-A leaders—problem solvers committed to making things happen and getting immediate results. They are willing to—and capable of—making the tough decisions, taking the necessary risks and persevering through hardships to get the job done. Sometimes *D*'s are too controlling and competitive for their own good, but when those tendencies are appropriately restrained, these people are major assets to an organization or ministry. They require the authority to act and thrive when given a broad magnitude of influence. *D*'s also tend to be suspicious of the motives and activities of other people, knowing that not everyone can be trusted and that what you see is not always what you get. On the negative side, their fear of being taken advantage of may lead to conflict or manipulation. On the positive side, their intuitive abilities dictate productive risks. You can minister to them by providing opportunities to use their decision-making skills, while helping them to develop greater levels of patience and understanding. Equipping them to calculate the costs of their decisions and to pace themselves and their colleagues better would also generate benefit.

One out of every five teenagers (21 percent) has the Steadiness style of behavior (*S*). These individuals like things to stay the way they are: Change and conflict are upsetting to them. They operate best when doing tasks that are low pressure and call for deliberate and well-planned action. Although they can be aggravatingly slow and rigid, they are good team members. They do not juggle multiple activities well, but they do a thorough job with the tasks they have taken on. They like being on a team, but they can be very hard on those who work with them since they often feel threatened and place the same demands on others that they feel responsible to meet. They also often respond poorly to new expectations or unstable environments, needing assurances of consistency and predictability. Loyal and kind in nature, individuals of this type are most productive when they are not rushed and when they can perform repetitive tasks. Guiding these people to adopt new behaviors takes time and patience. You can help them most by teaching them not to become paralyzed by details and by reducing their fear of the unknown. Because they are not good communicators, whatever you can do to help them communicate more frequently and clearly would be a step forward. Often "mousy" in demeanor, they will benefit from an increase in confidence and assertiveness.

Less than 1 out of every 10 teens (8 percent) is of the Cautious style (C). Accuracy means everything to these people, so they operate cautiously as a means of maximizing precision. Low-key in personality, they are self-motivated and detail oriented, and they are very conscientious about satisfying their standards of performance. They are critical thinkers and usually have a deep comprehension of their environment, expectations, resource base and challenges. They like to know the rules and to work within them. Their insistence on getting things done properly can be either a blessing or an irritating habit. C's are list makers and take pride in achieving their goals. Reflective, often creative and typically curious, they sometimes suffer from a perfectionist streak. They can be excessively demanding and even arrogant. You can help these teens to grow by affirming their accomplishments and by enabling them to be more realistic in their demands on themselves and others: Help them to loosen up and to "get a life." They are usually weak in skill areas such as delegation, conflict resolution, compromise and making decisions in a timely manner.

Our research within organizations has indicated that when each person's unique combination of these attributes is understood and utilized, every individual is capable of making a significant and fulfilling contribution to the organization. Just as Paul wrote that we are all given different gifts that add to the aggregate impact of the group when used properly, so does the appropriate use of people's personality traits and behavioral characteristics create synergy within the group and produce a sense of satisfaction and self-esteem.

We have seen, for instance, that people with the Steadiness style are rarely effective in a primary leadership position when the organization wishes to grow or become more dynamic. At the same time, we know that these individuals are indispensable partners to the charismatic, visionary leaders who are pushing the boundaries. Those characterized by the Dominance style are often dynamic leaders but are horribly miscast as counselors. Individuals of the Cautious type frequently shine in administrative and strategic development roles, but suffer when put into situations that require great flexibility and limited structure. They can be effective teachers because of their focus on empirical knowledge and comprehension and their need for precision in communication. Individuals with an Influencing style are typically effective at motivating participation and raising people's hopes, but they sometimes fall flat when required to create plans or to do desk jobs. Naturally, all of these generalizations have their limits, but understanding the type of individual you are seeking to minister to or work with can greatly enhance your impact.

In comparison to a recent nationwide survey among adults, we discovered that the personality profile of adults is considerably different from that of teenagers. Teenagers have a slightly higher proportion of Dominant personalities, a much higher percentage of Influentials, an equivalent percentage of Steadiness types and a much smaller number of Cautious people in their mix.

Whether this means that we can expect substantial behavioral transitions in the coming years as teens "grow into" the "typical" adult profile, or that the upcoming wave of young adults will bring a completely different nature to the national scene, is unclear. (The latter possibility seems the more likely.) If nothing else, however, the significant gap between the two groups (i.e., teenagers and existing adults) suggests that there may be increased conflict and misunderstanding between today's adults and tomorrow's adults as a result of such distinctive natural tendencies.

	Teens	**Adults**
Dominance	27%	20%
Influencing	45	30
Steadiness	21	24
Cautious	8	20

Further, these statistics serve as a reminder that each young person is a distinctive individual, imbued with special talents and gifts, as well as a unique style of handling reality. Acknowledging and comprehending such attributes would help us to more reasonably assign tasks and develop expectations, rather than to assume that all people are essentially the same. Our observation about organizations that utilize such insight is that they are able to build more effective relationships and communities, and to facilitate service activities that are more meaningful for both the served and the servants.

HOW THEY THINK OTHERS SEE THEM

There has traditionally been a gulf of misunderstanding between teenagers and adults. The research provides a sense of the contours of that gap from the perspective of teens. While adults, especially in the media, have a tendency to refer to teenagers as pessimistic, "slackers" and self-absorbed, teens resent such depictions. Given their own self-image—e.g., happy, responsible, optimistic, trusting, intelligent, religious, popular and emotionally sensitive—dealing with such an external image is, at best, an uncomfortable challenge to the average teen.

A majority of teenagers concurred that each of seven adjectives accurately depicts how adults think of teens. Tellingly, five of the seven adjectives are negative: lazy (which 84 percent of teens said was an attribute that most adults assign to teenagers); rude (74 percent); sloppy (70 percent); dishonest (65 percent); and violent (57 percent). The two positive attributes were friendly (63 percent) and intelligent (58 percent). In addition, about half (48 percent) contend that adults view teens as being pessimistic about the future.

Naturally, few teens view themselves or their generation in such negative terms. However, such a projection helps to explain why teens struggle with taking direction from, or being educated by, adults: They do not believe adults respect them, understand them or give them the freedom and creative license that they desire.

Notice how most of the positive attributes—trustworthy, family-minded, making America a better place, hard working and spiritual—reside at the bottom of the list. These five descriptions generated one-third or fewer teenagers who said those terms reflect an accurate portrayal of how adults view them.

HOW TEENS SAY ADULTS PERCEIVE TEENAGERS
(N=620)

lazy	84%
rude	74
sloppy	70
dishonest	65
friendly	63
intelligent	58
violent	57
pessimistic about the future	48
trustworthy	36
family-minded	33
making America a better place	31
hard working	29
spiritual	21

The ways in which teens believe adults perceive them are in a constant state of flux. Those views are also impacted by many influences, not the least of which is their own background and life stage. For instance, we found that younger teens have a more generous view of how adults perceive them (e.g., as intelligent, spiritual, family-minded, friendly and making America a better place), while older teens have the most severe view (e.g., as violent and dishonest). The ages of 15 and 16 are transitional years in which assumptions about their relationships with adults, as well as the assumptions regarding adult views of teens, undergo testing and change.

Another example relates to race. White teens were more likely than nonwhite teens to say adults perceive them to be friendly, but less likely than nonwhite teens to suggest that adults view them to be pessimistic about the future, trustworthy and violent. Nonwhite teens, especially blacks, perceive most adults to have negative views of them—which, in turn, influences behavior that may reinforce the negative stereotype held by many adults. In the race dimension we most clearly see these notions becoming self-fulfilling prophecies.

Faith commitment also impacts assumed perceptions. Teenagers who are born-again Christians were much more likely than other students to expect adults to describe them as sloppy and spiritual. More generically, teenagers who describe themselves as "religious" are much more likely than others to believe that adults view them as intelligent, spiritual and hard working, and less likely to be characterized as rude by adults. In this manner, the notion of being a religious individual has overtly positive connotations for one's self-image and associated behavior.

Interestingly, when adults and teens are asked to describe themselves, the profiles are very similar in many ways. In fact, the only significant differences are that adults are more likely to be optimistic about America's future—but not by much—and teenagers are more likely to be searching for meaning in life. Given their stage in life, however, the heightened emphasis upon discovering meaning in life is to be expected.

For individuals who interact with and hope to have a positive influence upon teenagers, these perceptions are of paramount importance, since they define some of the emotional barriers to overcome before a true partnership with kids can be developed. The issue, of course, is only partially whether or not teens are accurate in their assessment of the views of adults toward teens. Since these perceptions are real and they drive our attitudes and behavior, teens will react to adults on the basis of such assumptions, whether or not the assumptions are an accurate reflection of adult perceptions. Confronting the validity of those assumptions is a pressing issue for adults who seek to parent or minister to kids.

From the standpoint of those who wish to minister to and with teenagers, breaking down relational barriers and thereby gaining access and credibility will be imperatives. To get to that point may require adults to develop more realistic assessments of young people and more intentional and open communication about such matters.

The data also help to explain why so few organizations have effectively rallied young people around a vision, cause or purpose that might ordinarily appeal to young adults: more often than not, those organizations are led by adults perceived to hold negative views about teens and young adults. Without a sense of acceptance and respect, young people are not prone to submitting themselves to the leadership of people or organizations that have failed to embrace them as people.

Bridging the emotional gap between the young and old is not impossible, but it demands intentional and strategic effort to do so. A starting point is for adults to unconditionally accept young people because of their existence and potential, regardless of their behavior and values. The first step toward healing the generational cold war may be for parents to assert their love for their teens and to honestly reassess their views about young people. Other research we have conducted in the past several years shows that parents spend surprisingly little time in meaningful dialogue with their teens that is designed to build relational bridges and to work through conflict and mistrust. The solution to the perceptual gap is not more programs, more events or more materials but more time, communication and understanding.

POLITICS AT AN EARLY AGE

Relatively few teenagers believe that politics and public policy are the means to developing a better society. In fact, most teens have only a passing acquaintance with the key policy and political issues of the day—or even care to. This helps to explain why two out of three teens (67 percent) describe themselves as "somewhere in-between" the conservative and liberal ends of the political continuum. Just 15 percent claim to be "mostly conservative," and an equal number (13 percent) say they are "mostly liberal."

Far from the portrait that might be painted by the mass media, we found that born-again teens were only slightly more likely than were non-born-again teens to describe themselves as politically conservative. In fact, a small percentage of teen believers (21 percent) adopted that stance. Significantly fewer born-again teens (10 percent) described themselves as mostly liberal. The most important take-away, though, is that the vast majority of born-again teens also feel most comfortable in the less polarizing, gray zone of "somewhere in-between."

While the profile of born-again teens is often very similar to that of born-again adults, there is a marked difference between young believers and their elders regarding social and political ideology. However, this tendency seems to be true for all teens, not just the born-again group, and therefore may have no correlation with faith leanings. Note in the table below that born-again adults are twice as likely to call themselves conservative as are their teenaged counterparts—but also see that the same pattern exists among non-born-again adults and young people. What is most interesting is that for both the born-again Christian and non-born-again segments, the percentage of self-proclaimed liberals remains stable over time, while the proportion of conservatives increases from the teen years to adulthood. This also means that the pattern is one in which some teenagers who were middle-of-the-road in their ideological stance transition to a more conservative outlook as they age.

	Born Again		Non Born Again	
	Teens	Adults	Teens	Adults
mostly conservative	21%	38%	12%	26%
mostly liberal	10	8	14	17
somewhere in-between	61	47	68	49
base size	408	397	811	604

In spite of their tendency to be opinionated and to hold spirited discussions among themselves on the major moral and ethical issues of the day, most teenagers are not well-informed about the details of current events. Indeed, few teens refused to take a stand on controversial issues. The data also underscore the fact that in spite of their protestations to the contrary, teenagers may be somewhat more conservative than adults—and equally as ideologically confused as most adults.

POSITIONS OF TEENAGERS ON CURRENT POLICY ISSUES
(N=614)

Idea	Favor	Oppose
allowing students to pray in groups, before or after school, on public school grounds, if they want to	83%	14%
permitting public schools to teach creation as a theory of human existence	68	30
giving homosexual couples the same legal and financial benefits as those received by heterosexual couples	62	34
preventing the sale or distribution of pornography to people under the age of 18	62	37
not allowing women to have an abortion unless the life of the mother or the child is in danger	51	46
allowing a doctor to help a person who is terminally ill and wants to end his or her life to die by giving that person special life-ending drugs	50	49

Based upon our interaction with teens regarding six current or recent public policy issues, teens took a clear-cut stand on four of the six. By a six-to-one margin, teenagers endorsed the idea of allowing students to pray in groups, either before or after school, on public grounds if they desire to do so. By more than a two-to-one margin, teens supported the practice of public schools teaching creation as a legitimate theory of human existence. By nearly a two-to-one margin, teens affirmed giving homosexual couples the same rights and freedoms offered to heterosexual couples. And by a three-to-two margin, teenagers supported the prohibition of the sale of pornographic materials to minors.

The two issues on which teenage opinions were evenly split relate to the permissibility of euthanasia and abortion. As the accompanying table portrays, teens were slightly more likely to support a prohibition of abortion unless the life of the mother or child is in danger. However, our research generally shows that this is an issue on which people's opinions are fluid.

Why Teens Are Confusing to Adults

Have you ever had a conversation with a teenager in which you entered the dialogue confident of your own position and felt prepared to address whatever objections your teen counterpart raised—only to find yourself tongue-tied and intellectually baffled just minutes after engaging in discussion? In many cases we find it is not because the adult has failed to do his or her homework on the topics under discussion, but because teenagers have changed the rules of the game! Young people today think differently—the previously identified "mosaic thinking" style—and one result, when combined with their values and worldviews, is that they are abundantly comfortable with contradictions.

While their parents tend to focus on reconciling competing points of view—e.g., assessing blame, distinguishing between the appropriate and inappropriate, choosing the better of the options—young people are quite relaxed about the intellectual and emotional tensions that surround them. They are more likely to allow those competing elements to coexist without forcing a choice or developing a resolution. This comfort level is partially a function of their thinking style (i.e., a nonlinear approach, in which any route you take to any end point is equally valid) and partly a reflection of their comfort with diversity and inclusivity.

If you want to have a positive influence upon teenagers, it is important to understand the existence and relevance of these contradictions. Consider a few of them:

Teens are optimistic about the future, despite feeling unfulfilled in the present.
Only half of them feel "very satisfied" with their life today, and a majority contends that their elders do not respect teenagers. Without any particularly good reason for doing so, they believe life will get better in the near future, even though they are unable to explain why they feel this way. In fact, most of them feel that they are not adequately equipped to handle the future, yet they look forward to it with high hopes.

Most teenagers feel driven to achieve "success," although they are confused about meaning, purpose and direction in life.

In other words, they think they know the broad strokes of what they want—health, physical and financial comfort, education, family, friends—but they don't know the details of what it looks like or how to get there. They are committed to achievement without knowing if it even fits into that better existence for which they plan to strive.

Most teens are highly interested in spirituality, but comparatively few are engaged in the pursuit of spiritual depth.

They have eschewed religious games and institutions in favor of true spiritual meaning and living. However, by their own admission they are only minimally committed to their alleged faith of choice (i.e., Christianity) and to the spiritual practices that will supposedly lead them to spiritual maturity. They devote their time and energy to other, admittedly less productive pursuits—and show no signs of giving up either the hope of spiritual growth or their commitment to the pursuit of pleasure.

Millions of teenagers have been deeply wounded by their family yet most of them have a deep commitment to achieving family health in the future.

They have been hurt, but they are not giving up. They believe that the family is one of the mechanisms that will enable them to maximize their life. Although it has not been modeled for them, and even though our society is constantly toying with the radical restructuring of family foundations, teenagers anticipate having a strong family experience in the years to come: a good marriage, loving kids, a comfortable home and meaningful intrafamily relationships.

Teenagers are renowned for their relational emphasis, yet their pool of closest friends changes regularly.

As a group, we have seen that teenagers are more interested in people and in process than in profit and product. However, their loyalty to people is much thinner than would be expected. This everchanging roster of confidantes has not diminished the importance they attach to friendships, nor the significance of relational marketing, but it does raise many questions about their ability to form lasting, meaningful alliances for either personal or professional purposes.

Six out of 10 teenagers believe that the Bible is accurate at the same time that even larger numbers of them reject many of its core teachings.
The issue is not access to the Bible: Virtually all of them own or have easy access to a Bible. The issue is not exposure to the content of the Bible. Most of them attend church activities, have religious discussions with family and friends or are exposed to religious media. The problem is one of simple inconsistency: They either are ignorant of biblical principles or may know the Bible's viewpoint but consciously choose to believe something else. This capacity is fueled by their uncertainty about the nature of truth.

The parents of teenagers have the greatest level of influence upon the faith of teens, in spite of teens and their parents spending little time interacting with regard to spirituality.
This is one of the arenas of life in which teens look to their parents for guidance and substance but emerge unfulfilled and empty. Yet, parents do leave a discernible spiritual imprint on their progeny—primarily through modeling. Kids ask the questions and beg for answers; the responses they receive are tacit more than explicit, answers found in the behavior of their parents rather than their words of explanation. Few teens have theological discussions with parents, yet teens reflect the same theological views as their parents. Teens often wind up in the same type of church (theologically and denominationally) as their parents attended, in spite of an absence of pronounced pressure or encouragement from their parents to go to the same type of spiritual gathering.

Most teens acknowledge that gaining understanding into moral truth is critical, but relatively few take the time to arrive at a workable conclusion to the matter.

This is an issue that millions of teens say deserves serious reflection—but when push comes to shove, video games, movies, music, hanging out and other activities of the teen life push such reflection out of the picture. The result is that numerous decisions are made in a truth vacuum. Sure, teenagers express great interest in having integrity, moral standards and laudable character. But they have thus far avoided the sacrifice of time, energy and image to both consider the foundations of moral truth and its implications for their life.

What does it all mean? Simply put, what you see is *not* always what you get; effective youth work is *not logic based!* (Perhaps it never has been; all I can say is the evidence certainly suggests that teens are not always best understood through rational thinking and the expectation of predictable behavior.) Devoting precious resources in an attempt to reconcile these competing realities will likely prove to be an exercise in waste. A bigger picture of ministry, based on a deeper understanding of this age group, is required to facilitate transformative work.

The ministry strategies that have traditionally been used—even among the Buster teens as recently as during the mid-'90s—may not work today. The current teenaged population is operating with different fundamental assumptions about life. The mechanics of effective ministry must be more personal, more thoughtful and more networked than ever before. And, by the way, just when you think you've figured them out, do yourself a favor and don't bet on it. It is very easy to overestimate your impact, success and understanding of this group and the ministry efforts designed to affect their lives.

In chapters to come we will focus on the spiritual and moral dimensions of teen reality more closely. The challenge is for you to constantly examine the validity of your assumptions about teenagers. Know what you're striving to accomplish in your interaction with them, but also keep an open mind as you attempt to discern where they're coming from and how you might best influence them. Even the not-so-evident aspects of youth existence may be changing more quickly and radically than you ever imagined.

Note

1. Among the many assessment tools we have studied, one of the most useful is the Performax (also frequently referred to as the DiSC test), developed by Carlson Learning Systems. In our experience, as well as in Carlson's validation testing, this tool has proven to be remarkably valuable in determining core attributes that drive a person's response to different types of situations. Our own test is based on some of the principles discerned from the DiSC approach, and we have maintained the DiSC language to help ministry professionals translate their own knowledge of DiSC outcomes into ministry opportunities among teens.

C H A P T E R   3

MATTERS OF
THE HEART

One of the transitional traits of Mosaics is that they are relational, but are not as focused on people and relationships as were Baby Busters. They filter their decisions through concerns related to their ability to interact with others and their potential impact upon their peers. However, they are more likely than were their predecessors to weigh the competing values of doing something strictly to satisfy their emotional needs versus doing something to realize tangible or potential gains that are unrelated to relationships. In other words, to today's teenagers, relationships are important, but they are not everything—and they are certainly not the only things.

In fact, both the process and significance of developing and nurturing friendships has changed substantially in the last several decades. The perspectives and experience of today's teenagers underscore some of those differences.

FRIENDSHIPS

Most teenagers are realistic about the potential and the limitations related to personal relationships. For instance, the typical teenager claims to have just five "really close friends"—a much more reasonable assessment of personal bonds than was evident when Boomers were growing up. While some young people clearly have no idea what it means to have a "really close friend"—as judged by the assessment by some teens that they have 15 or more such relationships—the typical young person seems acutely aware of the emotional and tangible resources that close friendships demand.

In most cases those thought of as close friends are of the same gender as the teen, although roughly one out of the five close friends tends to be someone of the opposite sex. Black teenagers are notably different in this regard: they are much more likely than white or Hispanic teens to have two or more close friends of the opposite gender.

If the notion of diversity has not moved beyond lip service among adults, the opposite is true among young people. Most teens have at least one close friend who is from another racial or ethnic group. While that may not seem like a significant finding, remember that just a half century ago people of different ethnic groups rarely spoke to each other, much less befriended each other. Today, major communicators ranging from national advertisers (e.g., Tommy Hilfiger, Benetton) to politicians appeal to the racial tolerance of the younger two generations. It appears that such blatant allusions to racial diversity have a receptive audience among the Busters and Mosaics. The racial integration in our cities and suburbs, in athletic programs and in the music world, along with the recent surge in interracial marriages, has fostered such multiethnic friendships among teens. Add the high profile discussion of racial diversity emanating from politicians, religious leaders, athletes and entertainers, and the result is a generation of young people who almost assume that anything less is virtually illegal.

Teenagers walk a fine line between two primary sets of relationships: with their parents and with their peers. Not surprisingly, having their parents accept their friends is a major issue for millions of kids. Fortunately, most parents seem pleased with the friends selected by their teenaged sons and daughters. According to 6 out of every 10 teenagers, their parents approve of all of their closest friends, while another one-fourth reportedly approves of most of those friends. Few parents pass severe judgment on their kids' friends: just 7 percent of teens say their parents approve of only half of their friends, 6 percent say their parents accept only a few of their friends, and a mere 1 percent claimed their parents reject all of their friends.

The high rate of acceptance by parents may not be due to careful screening of those friends as much as it is due to ignorance. Only one-third of teenagers (31 percent) believe that their parents have taken the time and made the effort to get to know all of their closest friends; just half say that their parents really know most of their close friends. The age-old rap on parents—that they are out of touch with the people who mean the most to their kids—appears to be valid, since half of all teens note that their parents do not know most of their teens' close friends.

In defense of parents, though, realize that teens do not make this surveillance task easy for parents. Teens generally interact with their friends in neutral territory without parental presence—at malls, at sports events, in the hallways and lunchroom at school, at the movies or arcades, and so forth. Exacerbating the problem, teens also change their closest friends on a surprisingly regular basis. On average, about one-quarter of teens have retained their current circle of close friends without change over the past three years, one-quarter experienced a few changes in their inner circle during that time, and the remaining one-half of all teens admitted that their best friends represented a relational revolving door.

For a group of individuals who are so committed to the notion of experiencing long-term, enduring relationships, the rate of turnover among their friends is surprising. Part of this pace of change is attributable to the changing life cycle of teens, and part of it is due to the mobility of American families (i.e., a majority of households move within any five-year period). However, we also discovered that a significant share of this turnover is a consequence of the fluid nature of teen life: Change is the only constant, whether it relates to technology, schools, favorite musical artists, entertainment preferences or friendships. In some ways, teens (as well as their elders in the Buster generation) are more loyal to the *idea* of relationships than they are to specific relationships.

FAMILY MATTERS

Family is a big deal to teenagers, regardless of how they act or what they say. It is the rare teenager who believes he or she can lead a fulfilling life without receiving complete acceptance and support from his or her family.

The continued importance of family, in spite of the difficulties and challenges faced by families in recent years, is both expected and miraculous. One reason why we would expect such an emphasis is that one of the distinguishing marks of people born after the Boomer generation has been their insistence upon the importance of personal relationships. This focus has emerged for many reasons, not the least of which is a conscious rejection of the Boomer emphasis on achievement at the expense of people. (Many Busters and Mosaics believe in the importance of personal accomplishments, but they justify those achievements on the basis of how those outcomes benefit people rather than how they elevate the achiever.) Both Busters and Mosaics esteem relationships more highly than has been the norm for more than a quarter century.

In spite of the seemingly endless negative coverage in the media about the state of the family these days, most teens are proud of their family. Nine out of 10 (90 percent) consider their family to be "healthy and functional." This is an extraordinarily high figure given that one-third of the teens interviewed are living in either a "blended" or "broken" home—i.e., a home situation in which they are not living with both of their natural parents—and that a majority of those living with both natural parents harbor the fear that their parents may get divorced in the future.

TEENAGERS AND MOTHERS

Although millions of mothers of teens would faint at the idea, Mom is typically the most revered figure in the life of a teenager. Almost 6 out of 10 teenagers (57 percent) say they are emotionally very close to their mothers; 9 out of 10 teens contend that emotionally they are at least fairly close to their mothers. Some teen subgroups—most notably blacks, born-again teens, those who see themselves as leaders and those who believe they are very intelligent—are well above the norm in perceiving themselves to be emotionally close to their mothers.

Teens not only feel close to their mothers, but most of them have a substantial appreciation for how well she nurtures and raises them. When we asked teenagers what grade they would give Mom for her parenting prowess, three-quarters gave her an A, one-fifth awarded her a B and just 6 percent gave their mother a C or lower. While our research among mothers suggests that they would be shocked to receive such a complimentary rating from their young adults, teens possess an acute understanding that few people deem parenting a teen to be a reward that God bestows upon the righteous of the land!

The positive assessment of Mom does not mean that teens perceive their relationship with her to be perfect. When we asked teens to identify the one aspect they would like to change about their relationships with their mothers, one out of every three young people listed some aspect of improved communications. The most common improvements listed were having more open and honest talks, developing better understanding, and having less fighting and arguing when they interact. Other relational enhancements suggested were spending more time together and being given more freedom and independence by their mother (each listed by 10 percent of all teenagers). We also found that a substantial number of teenagers (3 out of 10) said there is nothing about their relationships with their mothers that they would change—some because they perceived those relationships to be very strong, others because they had never thought about the possibility that their mothers might change.

DESIRED CHANGES IN TEENAGERS' RELATIONSHIPS WITH THEIR MOTHERS
(N=620)

		Gender			Racial Group		Born Again?	
	All	Boys	Girls	White	Nonwhite	Yes	No
communication issues	32%	27%	39%	31%	35%	36%	30%
time together	10	11	9	11	8	14	8
freedom and independence	10	12	7	10	9	8	10
trust	8	7	8	7	8	7	8
specific behavioral changes	6	5	6	6	5	6	5
nothing	29	31	26	27	33	29	29

As might be expected, teenaged girls were substantially more likely than boys to desire an improvement in communications with Mom. Girls generally prove true to the stereotype of being more sensitive, more relationally focused and more affected by the amount of time spent with family and friends. When it comes to their ties with their mothers, teen girls are especially hopeful of improved communications.

TEENAGERS AND FATHERS

If the bonds between mother and child seem healthy and vibrant in the eyes of our nation's teens, the same cannot be said regarding the relationships between fathers and their teenaged progeny. Only 4 out of 10 teens describe themselves as emotionally "very close" to Dad; in total, three out of four say they are at least "fairly close." We found that teens who are from conservative families and teens who are most religious are the most likely young people to be close to their fathers.

Fathers are not rejected or unappreciated, though. While dads did not fare as well as moms on any of the measures we employed in our studies, neither did they fare poorly. One example is the grading on parenting skills. Overall, 6 out of 10 teenagers gave Dad an A, 1 out of 4 gave him a B and another 1 out of 6 gave him a C or worse. This curve is not as positive as that awarded to mothers, but neither does it indicate that there is a glaring gap between the perspectives of teens on their fathers as compared to that of their mothers.

When teens were asked to describe the single most critical change they would make to their relationships with their fathers, the most startling response was that one-third said they would not make any changes. The most common substantive changes suggested were the need to spend more time together (mentioned by 19 percent), wanting better communication (13 percent), discussing personal issues (7 percent) and spending less time arguing and fighting (6 percent).

DESIRED CHANGES IN TEENAGERS' RELATIONSHIPS WITH THEIR FATHERS
(N=620)

		Age Group			Gender	
	All	13-14	15-16	17-18	Boys	Girls
spend more time together	19%	19%	22%	14%	18%	20%
better communication	13	14	12	13	10	16
discuss personal issues	7	6	10	4	7	8
less arguing and fighting	6	6	4	6	6	5
his character or attitude	5	3	7	3	5	4
show more love, attention	5	5	6	6	4	7
spend less time working	5	3	7	5	6	5
be more understanding	4	3	5	4	4	4
physically present	3	3	2	6	3	4
nothing	34	34	31	39	38	30

An interesting transition happens in relations with fathers, in particular. During the middle years of their high school period, teens have a heightened need for their fathers' attention and influence. By age 17, however, a large proportion of teenagers begins to disassociate from their fathers, and their expectation levels decline accordingly. They seem less interested in spending time together and in discussing significant matters. This seems especially true among boys, as they prepare to become more independent after high school graduation. The signal to fathers is clear: If you have not connected in a resonant way with your teen by age 16, such a connection probably will not happen.

INFLUENCING TEENS

One of the greatest commendations awarded to teens' parents is that, of the 14 sources of influence we evaluated, parents were the only ones listed by most teens as having "a lot" of influence on how they think and act. More than three out of four teenagers (78 percent) acknowledged that their parents have a lot of impact on their thoughts and deeds. No other individual or people group came close to having that degree of perceived influence.

The impact of friends was acknowledged, with half identifying their friends as having significant influence upon their lives. Faith also emerged as a major influence, with half claiming that the Christian faith has a lot of influence on them, followed by 4 out of 10 mentioning the Bible as a major influence. Brothers and sisters were named by 4 out of 10 teens as major influencers, while one-third identified teachers. One out of 4 said their pastors, as well as the music they listen to, have a lot of influence on them.

You may be surprised to learn the identity of the sources of influence that teenagers claim have little or no impact on how they live. Some are realistically gauged by the teens, such as the influence of the Islamic faith. Others are more questionable, such as New Age religions, national political leaders and the information they get on the Internet. However, a few—most notably television and movies—are clearly underestimated by teens.

HOW MUCH INFLUENCE TEENAGERS ACKNOWLEDGE FROM VARIOUS SOURCES
(N=620)

Sources	How Much Influence They Have		
	A lot	None	Mean
your parents	78%	3%	3.68
your friends	51	4	3.32
the Christian faith	48	17	3.00
the Bible	44	15	3.00
your brothers and sisters	40	11	3.03
your teachers	34	12	3.10
church pastors or priests	27	17	2.69
the music you listen to	25	21	2.59
television	13	24	2.28
movies	10	31	2.10
New Age religions	7	55	1.73
national political leaders	6	43	1.93
the information you get on the Internet	5	49	1.73
the Islamic faith	2	82	1.27

Note: The mean is based upon responses that teenagers gave to each of these influences, using a 4-point scale that included "a lot" (value of 4), "some" (value of 3), "a little" (value of 2) and "none" (value of 1).

Among the interesting realizations emerging from this information is how much teens realize their parents influence them and how few indicated the magnitude of impact that the mass media have on their lives. Given the substantial amounts of time they spend engaged with the mass media, it is surprising that so few young people comprehend or are willing to admit the impact that television, movies and music have on their perceptions of reality, their values, their goals in life, their lifestyle choices and their relationships. Other research we have conducted has demonstrated the incredible power of these media to alter their opinions, attitudes, values, beliefs, relationships and lifestyle choices. Their failure to recognize or acknowledge that influence can be a dangerous blind spot.

Notice that among the highest-rated influences are faith elements: the Christian faith and the Bible were among the top five influence agents, while clergy rated seventh on the list. But who influences their faith views and practices? Once again, teenagers were quick to single out their parents. Half said that their parents have the greatest influence on their spiritual development, identified three times as often as the next most prolific source of faith influence (i.e., their church, named by 16 percent). Other spiritual influences mentioned included peers (8 percent), themselves (8 percent), relatives (4 percent), clergy (4 percent), God or Jesus (4 percent), their school (2 percent) and television (1 percent). In chapter 7 we will further explore the impact of parents on the religious behavior and theological views of teenagers.

SOURCES OF EMOTIONAL STRENGTH AND VULNERABILITY

In cooperation with KidsPeace, a non-profit organization that works with young people around the country, we explored how teenagers feel in relation to four core needs (safety, love, power and trust) and the provision of those needs by four key people groups in their life (parents, siblings, peers and teachers). We developed a series of indexes related to the four core dimensions (e.g., safety, love, power and trust) and calibrated teens' responses to a 100-point scale, with a range of 20 to 100. A 100 is a "perfect" positive rating, meaning that every teenager feels that the individuals within the group in question (e.g., parents, teachers, peers, siblings) provide perfect support all the time on that dimension. A 20 is a "perfect" negative rating, meaning that every teenager feels that the individuals in the group in question never provide the support the teen requires in relation to that dimension.[1]

Overall, the research revealed that teenagers feel relatively comfortable regarding the degrees of safety, love, power and trust they experience in life. The cumulative score suggests that they "usually" receive the kind of support they require to have a healthy and functional environment.

Parents Provide the Greatest Peace

Among the four key people groups, we found that parents have the greatest influence over teenagers. Confirming the generally positive ratings teens had given to parents in other surveys, in this study teens awarded their parents the highest marks for providing support in each of the four experiential dimensions (i.e., peace, trust, power and safety.) According to teens, parents do best at providing teens with love and safety but also do reasonably well at providing them with a sense of power and trust. The scores awarded to parents in these four areas suggest that while few teens feel that their parents do a perfect job in these dimensions, their parents usually deliver what the teen needs to maximize personal potential, to feel positive about themselves and to handle the challenges of life.

In rating their parents on 16 different indicators, teenagers were most likely to say that their parents do a stellar job of protecting them from sexual abuse of any type, providing love in all situations, protecting them from physical abuse and encouraging them to pursue their dreams for the future.

At the same time, teenagers indicated that their parents are not as supportive as they'd like regarding reactions to the quality of the teens' decision making, the value of the teens' ideas related to decisions the parents make and how well the parents understand the strengths of the teens. Teens also downgraded their parents for their failure to follow through on commitments made to the teens.

Teachers Are Helpful

Teachers ranked second to parents among the four influence groups evaluated, substantially lagging behind parents and placing moderately ahead of both peers and siblings in relation to the four needs. Teachers fared best in providing a sense of safety and were least skilled at providing love. They were moderately successful in terms of giving teenagers a sense of personal power and delivering trust.

Teenagers applauded teachers for protecting them from sexual and physical abuse, for encouraging them to persevere and for motivating them to pursue their dreams. Young people expressed disappointment with teachers for causing them to feel as if they are not important in teachers' lives, for ignoring the teens' ideas when the teacher makes decisions, for communicating that teens are worthless and for basing acceptance upon behavior, beliefs and achievements (i.e., conditional or performance-based acceptance).

PERFORMANCE INDEX
(by group)

parent safety	86.4%
parent love	84.5
teacher safety	81.1
parent power	78.9
parent trust	77.5
teacher power	75.3
sibling safety	74.4
teacher trust	74.3
peer safety	72.9
peer power	70.3
sibling love	69.9
peer love	68.9
sibling power	68.6
peer trust	65.5
sibling trust	65.4

Note: Each index was calibrated to a 100-point scale, where 100 is a "perfect" positive rating, and 20 is a "perfect" negative rating.

Siblings and Peers Rank Lowest
Siblings and peers generated statistically equivalent aggregate index ratings. Of the four key needs, siblings were best at providing safety and least effective at providing a sense of interpersonal trust—exactly the same rankings assigned to their peers. Notice that even though teenagers base many of their lifestyle decisions on input and reactions from their peers, teens are substantially more likely to describe their

parents and teachers as supportive than they are to describe their peers in the same way.

Teenagers were most appreciative of their siblings for protecting them from physical and sexual abuse. They were most disgruntled with their siblings because they perceive them to focus on the teens' personal weaknesses; for lying; for not protecting the belongings of the teens; for ignoring the teens' ideas; and for conveying a lack of worth of the teens.

Teens valued their peer relationships for protection against sexual and physical abuse and for the encouragement provided to pursue life dreams. The weakest aspects of peer relationships had to do with the failure to follow through on commitments made; lying; not considering the best interests of the teens; and for communicating that the teens are worthless individuals.

Finding Peace

Notice that the people with whom teens seem to experience the greatest peace are their parents—the very people, among the four groups tested, with whom they may spend the least amount of time. The individuals with whom they spend the most "quality" time—their peers—are the people who provide them with the lowest sense of peace. Perhaps there is more to the old axiom "absence makes the heart grow fonder" than we realize. (Keep in mind that the category of "peers" is different from the category of "friends.")

Also notice that the highest index scores were awarded to the two adult groups (i.e., parents and teachers). This seems to contradict teen expressions of emotional abandonment by adults. It may be the outgrowth of unspecified needs and expectations that they feel adults do not satisfy, even though adults are more highly regarded than are peers and siblings when specific behaviors are evaluated. Alternatively, we may be witnessing the effect of the changing of the guard from the Busters to Mosaics—that is, from the group that initiated the abandonment criticism to the group that has focused on other issues instead.

Overall, the higher scores in the four areas of key needs were most common among students who view themselves as secure or self-confident. The lowest scores were most likely among students who define themselves as angry, confused, lonely or skeptical. Interestingly, being "religious" seems to have little or no connection to achieving a sense of peace in life.

Thirteen and 14-year-olds had the highest peace levels; 15- and 16-year-olds had the lowest levels; and those who were 17 and 18 experienced a bit of a rebound. Perhaps the most remarkable outcome, however, was the minimal difference between age groups. Upon creating and analyzing 25 different indexes, we found that age emerged as one of the least significant variables. In other words, teenagers go through substantial turmoil during these years, but the degrees of power, safety, trust and love that they experience during their teenage years tends to change relatively little.

Boys exhibited a greater sense of peace with their parents than did girls on three of the four attributes (love, power and trust). On the fourth attribute (safety) the scores were nearly identical. However, girls had a higher peace index with the other three influence groups (teachers, peers and siblings) than did boys. Importantly, though, both boys and girls had a higher net score regarding their degree of peace with their parents than they had in relation to any of the other three influence groups. This may help the parents of teenage boys to relax a bit: What may seem like a boy's indifference to his parents may be nothing more than a level of comfort with his parents that enables him to focus on other dimensions of his life that require his energy.

Academic performance also emerged as one of the best predictors of a person's sense of peace. The scores for A students, compared with those of C or D students, were substantially different across all four influencer groups. Not surprisingly, academic achievement seems to facilitate a greater sense of peace in life, while poor academic performance correlates with a less-developed sense of peace—and the consequent struggles to compensate for that lack of self-esteem, comfort and sense of direction.

Note

1. For more information about KidsPeace, you can reach them at 1-800-257-3223. The information from this joint study was used with their permission.

CHAPTER 4

INSIDE THE HEADS OF TEENS

The teen years are deemed difficult by young people for many reasons, not the least of which is the plethora of challenges, opportunities, threats and decisions that confront youths. Having a chance to taste greater degrees of freedom and to make increasingly significant life choices raises the ante for teens—as well as their stress levels. Let's explore some of the dimensions they spend their time pondering.

MAJOR CONCERNS IN LIFE

One of the most surprising results of our recent teenage surveys relates to their identification of the major problems or challenges that concern them the most. Given the fragmentation within our culture, the multitude of serious problems facing Americans, the awesome array of choices available to young people and the impact of globalization, the expectation would be for teens to identify a virtual encyclopedia of concerns and problems that trouble them. Amazingly, quite the opposite proved to be true. The laundry list of worries that defined previous waves of teens has given way to a relatively compact list of issues. Less than a dozen issues represent a majority of the troubles acknowledged by teenagers.

By far the top-rated issue for teens these days relates to educational achievement. Four out of every 10 teenagers named the challenges related to educational achievement as their top focus. This reflects a major transition from just a few years ago. For teenagers in the Buster generation, educational achievement was seen as a means of arresting their parents' attention and gaining their approval. They were not thrilled about having to perform academically to win their parents' hearts, but they were desperate enough for love and acceptance to treat schooling as a major issue. Today's teens, driven by the Mosaic perspective, approach educational achievement from a different angle. The novelty of emotional abandonment by adults has worn off—in fact, we find that millions of young people, having been raised in such an environment, expect nothing else—and thus pursue educational achievement because they recognize it as a gateway to independence, self-definition and material success.

As a testimony to the importance of education, realize that three-quarters of all current teenagers (76 percent) say they will definitely attend college after graduating from high school, and an additional 20 percent say they will probably do so. This perspective is virtually unprecedented. Even students with an average or sub-par academic record, in addition to those who expect to go into trades or other non-professional work environments, plan to seek admission to college. Increasing numbers of high school graduates will start at the community college level, rather than in a four-year school, and millions of them will take five or six years to complete a Bachelor's degree. The underlying philosophy is that life without college leads nowhere.

Beyond academic achievement, the only three issues listed by at least 1 out of 10 teens were financial needs (mentioned by 12 percent, typically related to current family financial hardships), the stress and pressure of juggling multiple tasks and performing well (11 percent) and problems with friends (10 percent). The remaining issues named by at least 5 percent of teens included relational difficulties with parents (7 percent), relational difficulties with their family (7 percent), substance abuse (7 percent), time pressures and restraints (6 percent), career concerns (6 percent), physical threats (5 percent), personal financial problems (5 percent) and health issues (5 percent).

There's another way we can interpret this list. The chain of concerns is really comprised of three types of concerns. Topping the list is the potential to succeed in life, listed in various forms by nearly 6 out of 10 young people. Half as many (about 3 out of 10) identified needs and worries related to their physical and psychological well-being. The same proportion also identified relational considerations.

Although teenagers are concerned about the moral decline of the nation and the unappealing values they perceive Boomers and Builders to possess, less than 1 out of every 10 teens lists spiritual, moral and ethical issues as pressing personal concerns.

DEALING WITH THE FUTURE

Issues such as educational accomplishment and healthy relationships are significant to teenagers because they spend a substantial amount of time and energy thinking about the future. Half of all teens think about their future every day, and another 3 out of 10 think about their future several times a week. All told, 9 out of 10 teenagers ponder their future at least once a week. Only 2 percent claim to resist the temptation to daydream about what their life might be like in the years to come.

Thinking about the future is a natural inclination, especially for the young. But we discovered another motivation that compels young people to focus on the future: their concern about not being ready to handle the curveballs that life is likely to throw at them. Only 3 out of every

10 teenagers (29 percent) said they are very well prepared for the uncertainties and challenges to come. Most teens—about 6 out of 10—feel that their education, experiences and relationships have prepared them to some degree for what awaits them. It is this sense of being only moderately equipped to handle the future that leaves them feeling uneasy and restless—full of hopes, dreams and anticipation, but a bit fearful about their inability to master the coming challenges and unaware of how to better prepare to meet those challenges.

Despite feeling ill at ease about their future, teens have some clear ideas about how to get ready for the unknown. Not surprisingly, the top-rated bridge to success and fulfillment, in their eyes, is getting a college education. Half of all teenagers view a college degree as a necessary ticket to a meaningful life. One out of five teens (21 percent) expanded their view to express an interest in "life education"—that is, experiences, information, teaching and other resources that will prepare them for the realities of life after high school. Less than 1 out of every 10 teens listed elements such as job success, specialized skills, real-world experience, technological skills and solid relationships as the tools they will need to successfully handle the future. Even fewer young people—less than 1 out of every 20—named family support or religious maturity as keys to a viable future. One out of every six teenagers (16 percent) admitted to not having a clue as to what it will take to master the future.

PURPOSE AND POTENTIAL IN LIFE

One of the reasons why the future is daunting for many teenagers is that they are still working through basic considerations about the meaning and purpose of life. It is only natural to find so many young people feeling their way through the maze of possibilities regarding life's opportunities and striving to discern how such experiences relate to their reason for being. Despite physiological studies showing that young people mature more quickly today than in the past, and educational studies showing that elementary and secondary students are exposed to information and skills at increasingly younger ages, the teenaged years remain a major time of exploration, reflection and self-determination. Some things just cannot be rushed: Understanding who we are, why we exist, what we want from life and how to maximize our potential are areas of personal knowledge that resist overnight comprehension. Some outcomes require time and experience.

Three out of four teenagers (74 percent) concur that they are still trying to figure out the purpose or meaning of their life. This journey is affected by the fact that most of them—63 percent—admit that they do not have any comprehensive and clear "philosophy about life that consistently influences their lifestyle and decisions." Every day remains a period of discovery for them, a time to try new ideas, new behaviors and new relationships in their quest to solve the puzzle of life.

One of the disturbing findings, though, is that a majority (53 percent) contends that they have decided that the main purpose of life is enjoyment and personal fulfillment. In some ways this outcome is not at all surprising: It is exactly the same conclusion drawn by most of the parents of teens and is a perspective that is modeled and verbally communicated to young people by their peers and elders. Most parents lack any motivation not to embrace such a perspective; the absence of spiritual depth and moral reflection and their own philosophical superficiality support such a perspective. Hearing or seeing their offspring adopt the same perspective is therefore not a cause for chagrin among most parents, but rather a welcomed sign that their youngsters are finally maturing.

In their ruminations about meaning, purpose and direction, one of the encouraging results is that 9 out of 10 youths believe that it is still possible for one person to make a significant difference in the world. The issue they wrestle with is exactly how to do it.

The inner conflict over how to make life meaningful, though, is clearly seen in the struggle of teens to decide between two alternative foci: living for leisure or living for career success. Currently, teenagers are equally divided between seeing leisure as most important (46 percent) and seeing a career emphasis as the path to pursue (52 percent). This split also reflects the passing of the torch from the Busters to the Mosaics. Busters have been more focused on "life after 5," while Mosaics appear to be a throwback to the Boomer work ethic, prepared to invest themselves in career and other forms of life achievement.

GOALS AND ACCOMPLISHMENTS

To discover the relative priorities of teenagers for their future, we asked them to rate the relative desirability of 19 potential life outcomes or conditions. The results, displayed in the accompanying table, paint a fairly clear portrait of what matters to teens and how they currently view their ideal future.

Perched on top of the list of priorities is the attainment of a college degree. This was one of the five life outcomes that at least 4 out of 5 teens defined as "very desirable." Of equivalent value to teenagers are having good physical health, developing close personal friendships, having a comfortable lifestyle and having a marriage that lasts for the duration of their life (i.e., no divorce). Again we are reminded that their primary interests are relationships (friendships and marriage) and achievement (college degree and lifestyle comfort).

Three-quarters of the teen population rate the development of a clear purpose for living as a very desirable condition to pursue. This makes sense, especially in light of the high suicide rates of young people (i.e., the result of the inability to determine a viable reason to continue to live), the chaos in the world around them and the uncertainty of values and morals in today's culture.

THE LIFE GOALS AND PRIORITIES OF TEENAGERS
(N=605)

Condition	How Desirable Is This Condition?			
	Very	Somewhat	Not Too	Not at All
having a college degree	88%	10%	1%	1%
having good physical health	87	12	*	1
having close, personal friendships	84	14	1	1

Condition	How Desirable Is This Condition?			
	Very	Somewhat	Not Too	Not at All
having a comfortable lifestyle	83	17	*	1
having one marriage partner for life	82	13	2	3
having a clear purpose for living	77	20	1	1
living with a high degree of integrity	71	24	2	1
having a close relationship with God	66	22	6	6
making a difference in the world	56	36	5	3
influencing other people's lives	56	36	4	4
working in a high-paying job	55	38	6	2
having a satisfying sex life with your marriage partner	55	35	6	2
having children	54	34	7	4
being deeply committed to the Christian faith	50	29	9	13
living close to your family and relatives	49	40	8	4
being personally active in a church	43	39	8	9
owning a large home owning the latest household	28	47	19	6
technology/electronic equipment achieving fame or	27	46	20	6
public recognition	18	41	28	12

Note: * denotes less than one-half of 1 percent.

The next echelon of valued outcomes—personal integrity and peace with God—are not as crucial to most teenagers as are the tangible symbols and resources of success in this world. Nevertheless, 7 out of 10 teens are very interested in living life with a high degree of integrity, and two-thirds want to have a close relationship with God. What is equally intriguing about these desires is that as matters stand today, teenagers are not adequately equipped to accomplish either of these ends. Various studies among teens demonstrate that they appreciate the concept of integrity but have neither the knowledge of its substance nor a deep commitment to live with integrity. Similarly, while teenagers are enthusiastic about spirituality, relatively few have an abiding faith in God based on a true relationship with Him—and few have either the direction or inclination to pursue such a relationship, in spite of its conceptual appeal.

Slightly more than half of all teens said they are very desirous of making a difference in the world (56 percent) and influencing other people's lives (56 percent). These ideals go hand-in-hand, so their identical scores on the scale are not surprising. Certainly one of the means to impact and influence—as well as comfort and security—is through financial achievement, and 55 percent of all teens chose to prioritize the acquisition of a high-paying job. The other majority-stated goals were more familial in nature: having a satisfying sex life with their marriage partner (55 percent) and having children (54 percent).

Half of the teen population prioritizes a deep commitment to the Christian faith and living close to family. The former would require an increased investment of time and energy by teens.

Among the lifestyle outcomes that most teenagers do not prioritize are being personally active in a church (a top priority for 43 percent), owning a large home (28 percent), owning the latest household technology and electronic equipment (27 percent) and achieving fame or public recognition (18 percent).

Notice the relative positioning of the faith factors on this list. Two out of three teens are interested in a meaningful relationship with God, yet one-third fewer are geared to being active in a church. This is indeed reflective of the youth population's impressions of the local church: It sometimes has something to offer, but what it adds is neither consistent nor important enough to justify a significant commitment to such an entity. If they are going to find God, they believe they can find Him elsewhere.

When teenagers were asked to look ahead and identify the single most important thing that they want to accomplish with their lives, their ultimate goals tended to be completing a college education (20 percent) or making headway in a specific career they hope to have (29 percent). These two types of goals describe the dreams of half of the teen population. Other common goals included achieving a certain compensation level (12 percent), marriage or family objectives (10 percent), being able to live at a certain level of comfort and well-being (8 percent) and religious or spiritual development (7 percent). The pattern is unmistakable: American teens are much more interested in what they own or accomplish in life than in the development of their character. Given the cultural context in which they have been raised, this is not surprising.

EXPECTATIONS AND FEELINGS

If there was a time when teenagers were completely cynical about the nation, its future and their own place in that approaching period—and our own survey data suggest that we were immersed in such a period just a few years ago—then it appears that such a time has passed. Today's teens are grounded in reality but resolutely bullish on the future.

Earlier I noted that 9 out of 10 teenagers (89 percent) contend that it is still feasible to think that one human being can make a significant difference in the world. The ideals of youth, it turns out, do not end there. Nine out of 10 teens reject the notion that people who get married these days should expect to eventually get divorced. Eight out of 10 reject the idea that life is ultimately meaningless. Although most teens also argue there is no absolute moral truth, and we know that the basis of postmodern thinking and behavior is that consistent and knowable meaning no longer exists, perhaps the embrace of postmodernism is more by default than design—and, therefore, reversible.

Those who work in Christian ministry will be warmed by the finding that almost 9 out of 10 teenagers (88 percent) disagreed that "it is just not cool to be a Christian these days." The research affirms, however, that the label is not what makes being Christian cool—the essence of coolness is living as a sold-out, loving, compassionate follower of Christ. Teens possess a sensitive hypocrisy meter that is triggered by counterfeit faith. Truly living the life of Christ earns the respect of modern teens; talking up the faith but failing to live it is anathema to them.

It is disturbing to discover that 4 out of 10 teenagers (41 percent) could not think of any individual whom they respect enough to consider a role model. However, the flip side of the coin must provide some encouragement; i.e., that nearly 6 out of 10 teens are able to identify at least one human being whom they deem worthy of the label "role model." In most cases the individual whom they regard so highly is a family member.

GIVING AWAY THEIR RESOURCES

The expression of hope for the future, belief in the capacity to personally make a difference in the world, and their assumption that they can influence other people is consistent with their generosity toward people and causes. One out of every three teens donates some of their own money to a church or non-profit organization during a typical week, 4 out of 10 do so during a typical quarter, and not quite half do so over the course of an entire year. In other words, teenagers give away their resources consistently. Sensitive to hypocrisy, teens have made a good faith effort to live up to the ideals they wish their elders would affirm and apply.

Some might argue that it's easy to give away money in a culture of abundance. Perhaps a more volatile measure is how we give the gift of our time to individuals and causes in need. Americans tend to value their time even more highly than their money. To their credit, teens show a healthy willingness to give their time and energy to those in need. About 3 out of 10 teens volunteer some of their free time to help needy people in their area in any given week; about 4 out of 10 do so during a typical quarter. (The proportion changes little over the course of a year.)

Teens give to many of the same types of causes and charities as do adults. The big winners were organizations that engage in social welfare services or relief and development efforts (supported by 29 percent) and those providing medical and health-care services (23 percent). Entities focused on youth work and educational assistance also fared well (14 percent supported such agencies). Only 1 out of every 12 teenagers (8 percent) gave some of their own funds to nonchurch religious organizations in the past year. Organizations promoting environmental protection or animal rights were just as likely as religious nonprofits to attract teenagers' donations.

Even though teenagers want to reshape society and are willing to give up their time and money to have such influence, they are not yet committed to financially assisting the churches and nonprofit organizations with which they have had interaction. Only 1 out of every 5 teenagers (19 percent) indicate that they will "definitely donate" money to such entities in the coming year, with another one-third (35 percent) saying they will probably do so. However, a large segment said that they are not likely to donate in the coming year (21 percent) or that they are not sure they will do so (26 percent).

The tentative nature of teenagers' support of religious and charitable activity is exemplified by the fact that only half of those who said they are likely to donate in the coming year plan to give money to one or more of the same organizations that they have previously supported. There is a widespread desire to identify viable alternative recipients of their money.

As will be discussed in chapter 7, the unwillingness of teens to financially endorse churches and religious organizations with which they have contact is a further indication that they engage with those entities mostly to maintain personal relationships with peers of faith, rather than to have meaningful faith experiences.

As might be expected, born-again teens exhibited more divergent financial behavior in relation to ministries than did teens who have not accepted Jesus Christ as their Savior. First, a larger percentage of them gave money to nonprofit organizations (other than churches) than did non-born-again Christians (54 percent versus 38 percent, respectively). Second, the born-again segment was more likely to support organizations involved in social welfare and relief and development (34 percent, compared to 26 percent among non-born-again Christians) and to religious organizations (15 percent did so, five times the proportion of non-born-again believers who gave to such groups). Born-again teens were only half as likely as their non-born-again Christian peers to donate to health and medical organizations (15 percent versus 30 percent). Like their non-born-again Christian peers, however, they were just as likely to say they will donate again next year and were just as likely as their peers to plan to support the same organizations they supported this year.

MORALS, ETHICS AND TRUTH

Perhaps no issue is more important than a person's position regarding absolute moral truth. That perspective is the foundation on which a person's understanding of God, Scripture, core values, life meaning and personal behavior are based. It is reasonable to assert that the moral morass in which America is immersed is largely due to the widespread acceptance of relativism.

Over the years we have researched people's views on relativism and moral truth in various ways. Most recently we asked teenagers a series of questions designed to determine not only their stand on truth but also the intensity of their position and how they arrived at that view. What we discovered is both alarming and hopeful: alarming because of the current stand of most young people, but hopeful because few teenagers have solidified their position.

Although teenagers are twice as likely to embrace moral relativism as they are to accept the existence of absolute moral truth, the big (and best) news is that a majority of teenagers do not have a well-defined position on the matter. Overall, 3 out of 10 teens (29 percent) believe that moral truth is relative to the circumstances, while half as many (15 percent) say that there are moral absolutes which are unchanging. However, nearly half of all teens (47 percent) say that this is something they have never really thought about, and another 8 percent say they've considered the matter but have not reached any conclusion.

Let's turn to the teenagers who have taken a position on moral truth. If we examine how committed those 44 percent are to their substantive position (i.e., either to relativism or to absolutism), we see that among the

absolutists 63 percent are very certain of their position, while just 29 percent of the relativists are absolutely certain that their view is correct.
Interpreted differently, these figures tell us that 9 percent of all teens are
certain that absolute moral truth exists and 6 percent lean toward that
view but are not completely convinced it is right. Eight percent are certain
that moral truth is not absolute but is always relative to the individual
and his or her circumstances, while 21 percent lean toward that view but
are not convinced it is accurate. A majority does not really have an opinion on the matter.

   In some ways, then, the moral foundation of teenagers is still up for
grabs. Only one out of every six youths has a firm opinion on moral
truth. Given the importance of this issue, the tentative nature of most
teens' views should sound the starter's pistol for a focused scramble to
influence teen thinking on this pivotal matter.

   Keep in mind that although beliefs regarding moral truth form one
of the cornerstone philosophical perspectives of every human—and consequently exert an enormous influence on the culture in which they
reside—relatively few young adults reflect on this matter. Only one out
of every four teens (27 percent) said they had spent any time thinking
about this matter recently. While this may be sad or shocking, it is certainly not surprising. Americans are people of action and results, not
people of reflection, and teenaged Americans are no exception.

   Even though it may seem that few teens (27 percent) have thought
about morality, truth and absolutes, an additional bit of context drops
the figure lower still. We asked those who had previously thought about
the issue how important it is to them. A small majority of the 27 percent who had reflected on this issue considered it important but not
something on which they will spend much time or energy. Half as many
(one-quarter of the 27 percent) said this is an interesting but ultimately unimportant issue to them. Half as many again (just 14 percent of
the 27 percent who had thought about the truth issue) said this is a very
important issue to them and they consequently had spent considerable
time reflecting upon it. When projected over the course of the entire
teenaged population of America, this latter group constitutes just
4 percent of the nation's teens.

Discerning the existence of moral truth is so insignificant to most teenagers that half of them cannot even identify a source of information that has had the greatest influence on their thinking about the matter. The most commonly named influence was their family (21 percent), which emerged as the only influence identified by at least 1 out of every 10 teenagers. Other influences listed were religious teaching and beliefs (9 percent), the Bible (8 percent), friends (5 percent), life experiences and observation (5 percent), personal feelings and intuition (4 percent), and books they have read (1 percent).

We may conclude that teenagers don't think about moral truth often or deeply because they are neither challenged to do so nor is such behavior modeled for them. Their attitudes suggest that they have a sneaking suspicion that this is a vital issue, but without the people they trust and imitate devoting themselves to the matter, they have no trouble ignoring the issue.

Earlier I noted that teenagers are a study in contradictions. This characteristic arises again when we examine their truth views. When teenagers are directly confronted with statements about truth, their confusion shines brightly. Consider some of these inherent contradictions in their thinking about truth.

Seven out of 10 teens say there is no absolute moral truth, and 8 out of 10 claim that all truth is relative to the individual and his or her circumstances. Yet most of those same individuals—6 out of 10 of the total teen population—say that the Bible provides a clear and totally accurate description of moral truth.

Four out of five teenagers believe that it is unacceptable to break the law, even if no one is harmed by the infraction. Yet two out of three simultaneously argue that sometimes you have to break the rules or laws just to get by in life.

Three-quarters of teens agree that you can tell if something is morally right by whether it works in your life. At the same time, three-quarters assert that the Bible provides practical, defined standards by which we should live our lives.

The role of the Bible is clearly confounding to most teens. Not only are they evenly divided as to whether or not it provides absolute moral truths that are the same for all people in all situations, but their views on what the Bible contains in relation to truth are consistently inconsistent.

REACTIONS TO STATEMENTS REGARDING TRUTH
(N=614)

Statement	Agree	Disagree
When it comes to matters of morals and ethics, truth means different things to different people; no one can be absolutely positive that he or she knows the truth.	81%	17%
You can tell if something is morally/ethically right for you by whether or not it works in your life.	72	23
There is no such thing as "absolute truth"; two people could define "truth" in conflicting ways and both could still be correct.	70	27
To get by these days, sometimes you have to bend the rules for your own benefit.	66	33
The Bible provides a clear and totally accurate description of moral truth.	61	34
The way things are these days, lying is sometimes necessary.	59	39
The Bible provides absolute moral truths that are the same for all people in all situations, without exception.	49	49
The Bible does not provide practical standards for living in today's world.	26	72
It's OK to break the law as long as it does not hurt anybody.	17	83

Without a doubt, teen America's confusion regarding truth is a reflection of the distorted and contradictory teaching and modeling they receive from adults. The Church has provided little help in this regard: The teaching and exhortation provided to young people to focus them upon moral truth and ethical behavior is surprisingly infrequent and obscure, with limited accountability for the lessons conveyed. Some of the principles we teach are clearly grounded in a truth-based worldview, but that worldview itself is difficult to tease out of the larger body of information delivered in our preaching, teaching and relationships.

Unless teenagers are provided with a very different spin on truth—one that is comprehensible, relevant, compelling, practical and consistently modeled—they can be expected to follow the path of least resistance—which is the path of relativism.

THE POSTMODERN CHALLENGE

Much discussion has centered on the rapid movement of Americans toward the embrace of postmodern thinking. While this way of perceiving and dealing with reality is still in development, the heart of this philosophy is well chronicled. Busters flirted with it first, but Mosaics are absorbing its tenets without much deliberation.

Briefly described, postmodernism is a philosophy that stands in opposition to the scientific rationalism of the modernist era. Modernists believe that a person found meaning through personal growth and achievement; postmoderns contend that all striving is worthless and in vain since there is no meaning to be gained and no absolute truth to be understood. Modernists esteem knowledge and excellence; postmoderns would set their sights on comfortable survival and self-satisfaction. Relying on science and other tools, moderns seek to understand the order of reality and operate within those boundaries. Postmoderns claim there is no grand design, that all is based upon chance, and people therefore need not recognize the limitations and boundaries that circumscribed the world of the moderns.

The world of the postmodern is a universe that is decentralized. There is no ultimate authority beyond oneself; moral anarchy rules the day. How can the world survive in such a state of consistent chaos and selfishness? Moderns argue that there must be reason and intellectual honesty to create rules of fair play and to facilitate the potential for healthy coexistence. Postmoderns turn inward and suggest that the best decisions are based upon human will and emotion: Autonomous people will do what is best and work out the rough edges of those choices.

The keys to life comprehension are experience and emotion: Absent any kind of universal truth, the only reality that cannot be denied is what you feel or experience. Contradictions are therefore a natural part of one's existence and need not be reconciled.

Postmodern thinking does not assign value to knowledge for its own sake: Value is attributed only when the information has practical applications and is personally meaningful. Civility and respect for others is no longer assumed: In the postmodern view, someone earns his or her credibility and respect day by day, and few retain that level of acceptance for long. Even the notion of a hero is outdated under postmodernism—an insight that helps to explain why loyalty is minimal, and why star performers (such as rock bands and movie stars) have a short-lived walk of fame and celebrity these days.

Conversation represents the pinnacle of the postmodern experience. Communication is most effective with postmoderns when it is genuine: from the heart, vulnerable, honest, authentic. The use of stories is crucial when communicating with postmoderns because the narrative—especially if it is a personal confession or tale—cannot be denied or philosophically explained away. The more interactive the communication, the more effective it tends to be. Pedantic, factual, linear lectures are among the least effective methods of influencing how postmoderns think. The goal of communication with postmoderns is not knowledge, insight or discovery: It is participation, acceptance and belonging. This may bring greater insight into the changing nature of the ever-present world of entertainment. Rather than provide the audience with beauty, creativity, self-enlightenment or wisdom, postmodern entertainment is all about escapism, exploding accepted limits and exploiting technique.

In the postmodern world, spirituality is important but wholly personal. Because postmodern faith is centered on the person who possesses the faith, not the Being in whom that faith is based, faith is understood to be syncretic—that is, a personally pleasing mixture of whatever spiritual elements exist in the known world, resulting in an eclectic brew of beliefs and practices that help the individual handle his or her reality. For the sake of convenience, that faith may be given a known label (e.g., Christianity), but it is likely to bear little resemblance to that faith in its pure or intended form.

The absorption of postmodernism explains many of the contradictions, inconsistencies and transitions that define the latter half of the Buster generation and the entire Mosaic cohort. In fact, the acceptance of core postmodern tenets helps us understand why young adults can be so passionate about having faith, but so disinterested in the content of that faith.

Consider the contradictions between Christianity and postmodernism. Christianity exhorts people to find meaning in life through the practice of loving God and loving one's neighbor; postmodernism suggests that there is no real meaning to be achieved, so self-love becomes a reasonable, primary focus. Whereas Christianity recognizes the existence of moral absolutes as determined by God and conveyed through the Bible, postmodernism implores each individual to determine what is right and wrong for themselves, given the conditions, their feelings and their past experiences. One of the scariest aspects of postmodernism, from a Christian vantage point, is that there is no such thing as sin, since sin would have to be defined by moral absolutes. In the postmodern world, you can make mistakes and you can break laws, but you do not commit sin unless you choose to describe your actions as sinful. No external entity can characterize your behavior as sinful. Naturally, if there is no such thing as sin, neither is there the need for a savior or for salvation.

Christianity acknowledges the existence of one true God, who created all that exists, lives eternally and is holy, omniscient, omnipotent and omnipresent. Postmodernism encourages people to define their own understanding of God, based on their experience and perceptions, without the restraints that religious texts and traditions impose upon the human mind. To the followers of Christ, the death and resurrection of Jesus is the central episode of human history because it enables humans to be reconciled with God and have an eternal relationship with Him. Postmoderns accept that form of salvation as valid—along with any of several dozen other approaches to understanding eternal outcomes. Christians place their faith in God and the principles and teachings He delivered through the Bible. Postmoderns would rather rely upon themselves as the ultimate source of meaning, purpose and value. Because they live for the moment and have little anxiety about the future, the entire notion of eternal salvation is of little interest to them.

Chuck Colson once described the postmodern philosophy as one that could be summed up in a single word: "whatever." That has become the mantra of the emerging generation. Without any insight into the vacuous and dangerous philosophy that they have unwittingly accepted, teenagers are facing a rapidly changing world armed with a worldview that places them at the center, lifts up personal experience and emotion as the arbiter of decency and righteousness, and rejects historical experience as relevant to today's world. Postmodernism, unfortunately, is the perfect compliment to Mosaic thinking. And it will ultimately undermine the capacity of America to be a beacon of goodness, sanity, morality and purposeful faith.

As you interact with teenagers, listen carefully to the underlying basis of their ideas, their dreams and their reactions to opportunities. Most teenagers, we have found, have not thought deeply enough about these matters to understand the implications of the bits and pieces of postmodernism that they have embraced. Using a dialogical rather than pedantic approach, help them to explore their philosophy more thoroughly. The moment you excoriate their views as vacuous, shortsighted, improbable, inarticulate or baseless, you will lose their attention and openness. These are not matters that people choose to debate anymore; they will discuss them, but they will not engage in passionate, reflective arguments over such matters. Tread carefully in this minefield of philosophical confusion and emptiness, but be prepared to help young people explore the meaning of the meaninglessness they have adopted.

CHAPTER 5

WHITE, BLACK AND HISPANIC

Racial and ethnic relations is a public issue that predates the birth of the United States. In the days of the explorers, pilgrims and frontier pioneers, Native Americans bore the brunt of European and British arrogance and abuse. Blacks endured many years of prejudice and violence because of their skin color and historical roots. In subsequent decades various waves of European immigrants were received in America with open arms and mixed emotions. The influx of Hispanics and Asians during the past 20 years has again fanned the flames of racial hatred, fear and mistrust. Regardless of the principles embedded in our Constitution, we have proven that you cannot legislate morality and values, no matter how well-intended, foresighted or compassionate the leaders of a nation may be.

Historically, America's ethnic populations have been integral to the health and strength of our nation. However, the divergent elements of each group's unique culture—i.e., language, dress, relational idiosyncrasies, family patterns, religious practices, core values, symbols, heroes and lifestyles—have produced negative reactions within our dominant social groups. The result has been a residue of ugly events (e.g., police brutality, arson, name calling), distorted images and stereotypes, inappropriate marketplace reactions (e.g., job discrimination, price gouging) and gross cultural misunderstandings that have reshaped our national culture as well as each ethnic group's identity and cultural response.

As a predictable part of the push-pull forces in our society, the final decade of the last century birthed two related, reactionary movements that have been simultaneously caricatured as both divisive and productive. The diversity movement encouraged people to accept the breadth of ethnic and racial groups populating the nation as a reality to celebrate rather than lament. Proponents of this perspective have described diversity as beneficial because of the intellectual, emotional, spiritual and physical richness it adds to our social fabric. A related force has been the tolerance movement, which has encouraged Americans to exhibit a willing acceptance of people who have different characteristics, whether those relate to skin color, sexual orientation or socioeconomic status. While both of these views have significant merit, the practice has left much to be desired. The tolerance movement has inadvertently created new forms of intolerance through the imbalanced application of the underlying principles, almost as if to compensate for the unequal acceptance shown in the past. The result has been that several groups within our society—notably, evangelical Christians—endure more than their fair share of hatred and limitations in the name of fairness and equity.

Busters and Mosaics have been among the most avid proponents of diversity and tolerance. To their credit, they often practice what they preach, as evidenced by the diversity of their inner circle of friends, the growing proportion of interracial marriages and the widely held value of seeing beyond skin color to the essence of the individual.

At the same time, it is important to recognize that while young people may be quite accepting of peers from different racial and ethnic groups, there remain some very real differences among the young people from those groups. Hispanics, blacks, whites and Asians have very divergent worldviews, religious practices and beliefs, relational approaches, goals and lifestyles. None is necessarily better than the other—they are simply different.

Whether you are a parent whose teenaged child is dating a person of another ethnic group, an employer seeking to understand the ideas and communication styles of teenaged employees from divergent ethnic backgrounds, a teacher attempting to integrate a varied student body into a cohesive entity, or someone simply trying to make sense of news stories and random interactions with young folks from multiple ethnic groups, it may help to have some insight into how these groups are interchangeable and dissimilar. Let's take a look at some of those similarities and differences.[1]

DIFFERENT BACKGROUNDS

Not surprisingly, the demographic attributes of teens associated with each of the major ethnic groups are quite different. When people think about the teenaged population, our impressions are based upon a mixture of perspectives that borrow images and experiences from each of the ethnic groups, but most often we assign the characteristics of white teens to the entire teenaged population. This is mostly because they represent two-thirds of the teenaged population, and we are therefore most likely to observe, interact with and hear about that group. As dominant as white teens are numerically, though, they certainly do not fully represent the background and life experience of all other teens.

Teenagers are a product of the world in which they live. Elements such as their families, the types of schools they attend, the neighborhood in which they live and the media to which they have regular exposure affect them deeply. While social scientists are divided regarding the magnitude of effect that one's cultural and family surroundings have upon a young person's perceptions, core values and lifestyle choices, few dispute that the effect is highly significant. Whites, blacks, Asians and Hispanics typically have divergent advantages and disadvantages based upon their unique influences.

For instance, among today's teenagers, barely 1 out of 10 whites lives in poverty, compared to 1 out of 4 black and Hispanic teens. While the average white teen lives in a family that earns more than $40,000 annually, the average Hispanic family brings in slightly less than $30,000, and the average black family earns around $25,000. The differences are closely related to educational achievement. One-third of the parents of white teenagers have a college degree. That's double the proportion among blacks and triple the percentage among Hispanic parents. Because behavioral modeling leaves such a deep imprint on the minds of young people, breaking the economic patterns within the black and Hispanic populations has been quite challenging.

Marriage and parental status represent a similar area in which the differences among the ethnic groups are broad and deep. Two-thirds of all white teens (69 percent) live with both of their natural parents. The same claim can be made by only half of the black (46 percent) and Hispanic (52 percent) teens in America. Among the teens who do not live with both birth parents in the same household, whites are most likely to live with a single parent (usually the mother) or with a remarried parent; blacks typically live with a single mother and other relatives; and Hispanics are most likely to live with a single mother. Again, the impacts are dramatic, as evidenced by various studies that show children raised in single-parent households have a higher likelihood of getting divorced, experiencing physical and emotional abuse and abusing their spouse and children. They also are less likely to reach or exceed the nation's average family-income level. Genetics and upbringing are not inescapable shackles, but they do leave an unmistakable impression upon the lives of young people.

The stability of their home life also relates to the permanence of their residence. According to white teenagers, 90 percent live in a home their parents own. Only 10 percent say they are living in a rented residence—miniscule compared to the 29 percent of Hispanics and 36 per-cent of blacks who live in a rented residence. There is nothing inherent-ly wrong or problematic with living in a rented home, of course, but those who do so have higher transience levels, which impacts the rela-tionships, sense of stability, academic performance, extracurricular involvement and self-image of the young person who moves with his or her family.

Location is another distinctive across the groups. A majority of black and Hispanic teenagers live in urban areas, while just one-quarter of whites live in a city environment. Among other things, this impacts teen safety. Federal government statistics report that a black teenager is cur-rently five times more likely to die from a gunshot wound than is a white teenager. This parallels the patterns of crime and violence that distin-guish cities, suburbs and rural areas in general.

Keep in mind that "different" does not always indicate that some-thing is inferior or undesirable. The fact that the family dynamics, household experiences and cultural environments of blacks and Hispanics are substantially different from those of whites does not mean that they are missing out on an idyllic reality. The issues raised by information that describes the differences relate to understanding those differences and their implications and reflecting upon the provision of opportunities to change, should such a shift in experiences be desired.[2]

LIFESTYLES DIFFER

Not surprisingly, given their divergent family and household traits, as well as their environment, the three largest teenaged ethnic groups also have some visible differences when it comes to how they spend their time and money.

Recent governmental studies show that ethnicity has little to do with eating habits: Teenagers of all colors and backgrounds have mediocre diets! In fact, one recent study concluded that only 6 percent of teenagers have a healthy diet.

Roughly one-quarter of each group admits to having used illegal drugs in the past year, and a similar proportion admits to having consumed an alcoholic beverage in the past month. Numerous studies have suggested that beyond the physical impact that drugs have on a young person, the act of voluntarily taking drugs is indicative of a mind-set that more often than not results in lifestyle choices that produce a plethora of economic, relational and physical hardships. In the short-term, the regular use of drugs tends to have a negative influence on the relational circles of teens, while depleting their financial resources.

Consuming alcoholic beverages follows a similar pattern as that of drug use: about one-quarter of all teens drink beer, wine or mixed drinks in a typical month. About 1 in 10 consumes enough alcohol to get drunk at least once during a typical month. The older the teen becomes, the more likely this tendency is, regardless of ethnic group.

Music remains one of the seminal influences in the lives of young people, though we also discovered that less than one out of five teens admits that music impacts their thinking or behavior. The musical preferences of the three largest ethnic subgroups are quite divergent. White teens prefer rock and pop music; blacks are partial to rap, hip-hop and R&B; Hispanics favor rap. Musically, one of the few points of agreement across the three groups is a common distaste for country music. Country emerged as the most widely disliked musical genre for whites, blacks and Hispanics.

The influence of music is underscored by the fact that three-quarters of whites and blacks, and two-thirds of Hispanics, had purchased musical recordings in the past year, with a typical teen buying an average of 7 to 10 recordings. Relatively few of those purchases included Christian music: Only about one-fifth of teens bought a Christian recording within the past year. When they did, again we found huge differences in taste. Whites were most likely to buy worship compilations and DC Talk. Black teens preferred black artists, such as Kirk Franklin and Yolanda Adams. Hispanic teens turned to artists such as Jackie Velasquez, the Supertones and Jars of Clay.

All of these influences have certainly impacted the life goals of teens. The future is a much bigger concern among nonwhite teens than among their white peers, partly because white teens have been raised in relatively affluent, comfortable environs and thus feel less anxiety about how they will make their way through the complexities of the unknowns that await them. Overall, only 2 out of 10 white teens said they think about their future every day; two-thirds of black teens and half of the Hispanic teens consider their future on a daily basis. Few teens feel well prepared for the future, but whites were about one-third more likely than nonwhite teens to have a comfort level about the future. To be better prepared for the coming challenges of life, by far the most common perspective of teens, regardless of their ethnic group, was to complete a college education. Effective preparation was more likely to include job experience in the minds of Hispanics and technological expertise or other specialized skills in the eyes of blacks.

What images fill the minds of young America as it dreams of an ideal future? Each ethnic group pieces together its dream future a bit differently. Among white teens, the keys are good health, close friends, a solid marriage, a college degree and a comfortable lifestyle. Among black teens, the preferred future is defined by good health, a close relationship with God, a clear purpose for living, a comfortable lifestyle, a high-paying job, living with integrity and a college degree. Hispanic teens look forward to good health, a college degree, a comfortable lifestyle, close friends, a good marriage and a clear life purpose.

The differences among the three groups are revealing. Whites are the group least concerned about the role of faith in their life and most worried about the strength of their marriage. They are the most focused on their network of friends, but least concerned about the long-term relationships they maintain with family. Blacks show the greatest interest in faith, integrity, purpose, financial achievement and sexual fulfillment, and the least interest in having a single marriage for life. Hispanics, compared to other teens, exhibited the greatest interest in lifestyle comfort (including a large home and a big salary) and in living close to family and relatives. Purpose, integrity, influence and faith were comparatively unimportant to them.

The dominant life issues and challenges each group identified as the major obstacles to enjoying their lives support those distinctions. In the eyes of white teens, the big threats in life relate to the inability to get the education they want and tensions in their existing relationships.

Both black and Hispanic youths saw the major challenges in terms of educational achievement, personal economic choices and opportunities, and the threat of physical violence. Don't lose sight of the fact that teens, regardless of ethnicity, did not view world conditions, morality, faith or health as major challenges to be addressed as they seek to experience their ideal life.

RELATIONSHIPS

Relationships have varying degrees of importance within the ethnic communities. Overall, we found that friendships are most cherished by white teens and least cherished by Hispanic teens, with blacks straddling the line between these groups. Nonwhite teens were slightly more likely to describe themselves as lonely, yet they consistently showed less passion for building lasting, deep friendships with their peers. This may well be related to the revelation that although family relationships are important to all three groups they were most highly prized by nonwhites.

Intriguingly, only half of all teenagers (49 percent) said that all of their really close friends are of the same racial group as they come from. In other words, about half of all teens identified at least one close friend who is from another racial or ethnic group. So their relationships are not dependent upon racial or ethnic ties, a relatively new phenomenon. Keep in mind that although America has always been a melting pot of ethnicity, in the past it was rare for people of different ethnic backgrounds to have close relationships with one another. While Boomers may have initiated a move toward racial tolerance, Busters advanced matters by intentionally pursuing racial harmony, and Mosaics are likely to keep moving down the same path. So while adults are talking about its importance, racial diversity has become a reality in the world of the younger two generations.

Family relationships are central to the self-confidence and self-image of most teens. Within the family, teens' mothers emerge as the most revered figure, with nearly 3 out of every 5 teens (57 percent) saying they are emotionally very close to their mothers and only 10 percent claiming to be either not too close or not at all close to their moms.

Black teens (71 percent) were much more likely than others (54 percent) to describe themselves as being emotionally very close to their moms. Hispanic teens were much more likely than either white or black teens to cite communication issues as their top priority related to improving their bonds with their mothers (listed by 40 percent of Hispanics and 30 percent of white and black youths). Black teens were three times more likely than white teens to identify the desire to talk about personal issues.

Concerning their fathers, most teens also respect and want meaningful relationships with their dads. Black teens were three times more likely than white teens to want their fathers to express their love for them. White teens were twice as likely as nonwhite teens to want their fathers to devote less time to work. Surprisingly, receiving greater understanding and having better communication were interests of white and Hispanic teens but not of black teens. Overall, 19 percent of whites and 23 percent of Hispanics, but just 6 percent of African-American teens listed these two types of changes as desired changes.

TEENS AND TECHNOLOGY

A study conducted by The Barna Institute regarding teenagers, technology and faith revealed some intriguing realities.[3] It is important to know that computers and the Internet are an ingrained element in the lives of most teens these days. In early 2001, we found that 9 out of 10 teenagers, regardless of their ethnicity, have used the Internet. Although white teens use the Net more often (about half use it daily, compared to one-quarter of black and Hispanic teens), most teenagers are Net-conversant and feel comfortable turning to the Internet for information and other benefits.

The ways ethnic groups use the Internet vary slightly. Overall, the Net is used to deliver information, preview music and videos, facilitate relationships, and access games. However, whites, who consistently emerge as much more relationally focused than blacks or Hispanics, are twice as likely as other teens to rely upon the Internet to maintain existing relationships and are currently much more likely to use the Net for spiritual experiences. Whites also have a 30 percent higher likelihood of using the Net to buy products. Blacks were distinguished by having the highest probability of using the Internet to explore new music or to watch video clips online. They were also the segment most likely to download or to play video games online. Hispanic teens were the group most attracted by online chat, and least enticed by music, videos, video games and faith experiences.

WHAT TEENAGERS USE THE INTERNET FOR THESE DAYS
(N=605, 9/00)

	White	Black	Hispanic
to find information	92%	99%	90%
check out videos, new music	62	76	49
maintain existing relationships	49	26	22
engage in online chat	42	47	58
play video games	38	43	31
make new friends	37	30	31
buy products online	31	22	22
have a religious/spiritual experience	14	7	2

The Internet is viewed as a source of faith experiences with moderate interest by all three teen segments. Although relatively few teenagers expect to abandon the physical church in favor of a cyberchurch or solely online faith commitment, their openness to having faith-related experiences online is extraordinary. Large percentages of teenagers expect to use the Internet in the near future to have faith chats, read motivational or devotional writings, submit online prayer requests to a cybercommunity, listen to religious teaching that can be downloaded or audio-streamed, and buy religious music.

Just 1 out of 10 white teens plans to use the Internet for all of their religious and spiritual experiences and learning in the future. That's much less than the 2 out of 10 black teens and 1 out of 4 Hispanic teens. The implication, of course, is that the traditional church is part of the white culture in America, but that teens of color are increasingly open to experiencing and interacting with God in various ways—including a digital format. Given their frustrations with the physical church, it is not odd to notice that Hispanic teens, in particular, are warming up to the idea of "doing church" online. Our earlier findings noted that Hispanic teens tend to be family-oriented but are typically less relational than are white or black teenagers. Establishing themselves as the group most likely to depart from a physical community of faith fits that profile.

HOW TEENS PLAN TO USE THE INTERNET
FOR FAITH IN THE FUTURE
(N=605)

Statement	White	Black	Hispanic
submit prayer requests to a group that prays for people's needs	50%	68%	52%
read a short, religious reading to motivate, challenge or focus	55	50	55
listen to religious teaching contained in an online archive of teaching that you could access whenever you want, on whatever topic is of interest to you	50	42	57
participate in a chat room or discussion forum about religion or faith	46	43	55
participate in a real-time, online Bible study	33	42	47
buy books or study guides about religion/faith	38	39	43
participate in an independent study course on faith matters	38	48	34
buy religious music	36	42	35
be mentored or coached in spiritual development by a person whose faith is more developed than yours	36	33	34
participate in an online class that meets regularly online to study some aspect of faith or religion	28	23	42
worship God through a real-time, video-streaming worship experience	21	26	13

ATTITUDES AND MIND-SETS

The worldviews and core attitudes of teens vary according to their ethnic affiliation. Understanding these views is useful because such perspectives shape a person's values and behavior.

Focusing upon the differences in their outlook on life, we find that whites are more likely to claim that the purpose of life is enjoyment and personal fulfillment, and to believe that there is no absolute moral truth. They are the least likely to believe that to get by in life you have to bend the rules to your personal benefit (although three out of five accept this idea as appropriate). Most white teens, unlike their peers from other ethnic groups, believe that euthanasia should be legalized.

Black teens were the most likely to accept situational ethics (i.e., you know if something is morally or ethically right if it seems to work in a situation). They were the least likely of the three ethnic groups to say that moral truth cannot be known with certainty or that there is no absolute moral truth, and to argue that the purpose of life is enjoyment and personal fulfillment. Black teens were most likely to support public schools teaching creationism, and least likely to favor gay couples receiving the same legal and financial benefits as heterosexual couples. They were half as likely as Hispanic teens, and just one-third as likely as white teens, to support euthanasia.

Hispanic teens were twice as likely as other teenagers to believe that it is acceptable to break the law as long as nobody gets hurt in the process. They were also twice as likely as others to argue that people who get married these days should expect their marriages to end in divorce. Hispanic teens topped the list in saying that lying is sometimes necessary: two-thirds contend that this is reality. They were only half as likely as others to say that satisfying leisure is more important than having a satisfying job or career. Hispanic teens were also noteworthy for being substantially less likely than white or black teens to block the sale of pornography to minors, and they were least supportive of students being allowed to voluntarily pray at school.

Another aspect of the behavioral differences among the three groups is underscored by the results of the inventory they completed for us.

We discovered that white and black teens are very similar in terms of their likelihood to fit within each of the four groups described in chapter 2: Influencing, Steadiness, Cautious and Dominant. Hispanic teens were very different in their profile. They were about half as likely to fit the Dominance profile; more than twice as likely to fit the Cautious category; slightly less likely to meet the criteria for the Steadiness classification; and half of them fit the Influencing style. In other words, half of all Hispanic teens were evenly divided among the first three categories, and the remaining half were in the Influencing group.

The practical implication of this outcome is that Hispanic teens are more likely to rely upon their personality to make progress in life. They are more likely than their peers to be spontaneous in their decision making, to rely upon stream-of-consciousness conversation when solving problems and to be enthusiastic and optimistic in their approach to people and situations. Hispanic teens are not highly relational, yet they are highly interactive. They are sensitive and emotional in their engagement with others, but less likely to seek control, authority or consistency with the past.

FAITH PRACTICES

The faith dimension of teens varies dramatically according to their ethnicity. Although most of them describe themselves as Christians, what that means to them and how they practice their faith varies considerably across the three main ethnic groups.

A clear distinctive relates to their church affiliations. Half of the whites associate with evangelical Protestant churches, and one-quarter attend mainline Protestant churches. Half of all blacks are aligned with Baptist churches. About half of all Hispanic teens are affiliated with the Roman Catholic church.

Faith practices vary, but perhaps not as substantially as might be imagined. White and black teens had a very similar profile of faith practices. Whites were substantially less likely than blacks to donate their own money to a church during a typical week, but otherwise the activity levels are similar. Hispanics, however, vary significantly on several fronts. Compared to both white and black teens, Hispanics were less engaged in virtually every spiritual endeavor tested: worship service attendance, Sunday School attendance, small-group involvement and youth-group participation. They were also somewhat more likely to read from "sacred literature" other than the Bible.

TEENS' FAITH PRACTICES ENGAGED IN DURING THE PAST SEVEN DAYS

Statement	White	Black	Hispanic
attended a Christian church worship service	55%	57%	47%
attended a Sunday School class	40	36	30
prayed to God	86	87	86
participated in a small group that meets regularly for Bible study, prayer or Christian fellowship, not including a Sunday School or 12-step group	30	25	22
read from the Bible, not including while at a church	35	35	31
attended a church youth group activity or event other than a small group or Sunday School class	35	33	22
read from a sacred text or book other than the Bible	21	18	27
donated any of your own money to a church	34	57	39

Youth groups are attended by about one-third of America's teenagers. The reasons behind that involvement parallel some of the other patterns we have already identified regarding their values and lifestyles. For instance, among white teens, the major reason they attend is because their friends are there. Among black teens, there is an equal pull to be present because of their friends and because they would like to learn more about God. Hispanic teens, who are the least likely to attend youth group meetings and attend with less frequency than do white and black teens, are drawn primarily by the content that is delivered in those meetings.

Black teenagers also demonstrated a much greater tendency to attend multiple churches rather than to always attend the same church: half do so now, compared to one-third of white and Hispanic teenagers. However, the most important insight is to recognize that large—and growing—numbers of teenagers feel little loyalty to any one church.

Increasingly, they attend whatever church seems to fit their needs at the moment. This will undoubtedly affect the way that churches strive to build community and momentum in the future.

Further affecting the health and stability of the Church in the years to come is the low likelihood of a teen's remaining churched. Barely one-third of white and Hispanic teens, along with two-fifths of black teens, say they are likely to continue to attend a Christian church in the future, when they are living independent of their parents.

Even the factors that teenagers deem important in a church vary across ethnic lines. When we had teens evaluate the importance of each of 16 attributes of churches they might choose to attend, we learned that white teens are least likely to consider the distance of the church from their home, whether the church helps the poor or not and the quality of the adult Sunday School classes. Blacks are more likely to consider the quality of the sermons, the breadth of ministry programs available, the beliefs and doctrine of the church, the quality of the music in the worship events and the quality of the Sunday School program for adults. They are relatively less likely to be concerned about how friendly the congregation is toward visitors. Hispanics distinguish themselves by being more concerned about having people their own age and how many of their good friends attend the church. Hispanics demonstrated a much lower threshold of interest than whites or blacks in matters such as the type or amount of music in worship events, the degree to which congregants care for each other, the beliefs and doctrine of the church, how much they like the pastor or the times of the services.

WHAT TEENS BELIEVE

When you study the faith beliefs of teens, one thing becomes quite clear: whites, blacks and Hispanics have very different views on biblical and spiritual matters.

Actually, whites and Hispanics operate on pretty much the same wavelength regarding most matters of doctrine. The only distinctions of note between these two groups are that Hispanic teens are more likely to describe Jesus Christ as a sinner and more likely to believe that a good person can earn a place in heaven and that God is no longer directly involved in our world. Hispanic teens were also less certain of their theology, as a lower percentage of them said they are very familiar with all of the major principles and lessons of Christianity. To their credit, they were also less likely to assert that their beliefs will not change in the future.

The eye-opener relates to the belief chasm between blacks and other teens. Among the three major ethnic segments, black teenagers have a belief profile that most closely resembles the teachings in Scripture. As you can see by studying the distinctions between whites and blacks shown in the accompanying table, black teens have a better understanding of sin, judgment, salvation and the validity of Scripture. Black teens also have a more orthodox view of God and are more likely to be born again (42 percent, compared to 34 percent of whites and 24 percent of Hispanics).

Specifically, we found that compared to other teens black teenagers are more likely to believe in God's judgment of all people; that the miracles described in the Bible happened; that forgiveness of sins is possible only through Christ; that the Bible is totally accurate in all it teaches; that the Bible defines absolute moral truths for us; that without Christ, a person is condemned to hell. They are comparatively less likely to believe that sin is an outdated concept and that there are some sins that God cannot forgive. Even some key attitudes regarding behavior are different. Black teens are more likely to state that their behavior has been changed by their beliefs, that it is important to be a church member and that they have a personal responsibility to share their faith, as well as being less likely to indicate that they lack a philosophy of life that influences their lifestyle.

WHAT TEENS BELIEVE
(N=1219; percentages are teens who agree with statement)

Statement	White	Black	Hispanic
Your religious faith is very important in your life.	81%	85%	77%
Your religious faith has helped you, personally, to have a greater sense of peace.	81	84	85
The Christian churches in your community add real value to the life of the community.	77	78	75

Statement	White	Black	Hispanic
The Bible teaches that God helps those who help themselves.	75	72	76
Your religious beliefs are not likely to change in the future.	75	78	62
All people will be judged by God after they die, regardless of their religious beliefs.	71	85	66
All of the miracles described in the Bible actually took place.	71	94	78
The Christian faith is relevant to your life today.	71	77	68
You feel that you are very familiar with all of the major principles and teachings of the Christian faith.	69	67	56
You can think of specific times recently when your religious beliefs actually changed the way you normally would have behaved.	67	85	63
God is the all-knowing and all-powerful perfect creator of the universe who still rules the world today.	67	80	63
The devil, or Satan, is not a living being but is a symbol of evil.	64	66	67
You have not yet developed a clear philosophy of life that consistently influences your lifestyle and choices.	64	58	68
You feel it is important for you to be a member of a church.	63	81	67
If a person is generally good, or does enough good things for others during his or her life, he or she will earn a place in heaven.	60	57	71
Forgiveness of sins is only possible through faith in Jesus Christ.	59	83	56
The Bible is totally accurate in all of its teachings.	59	74	64
You, personally, have a responsibility to tell other people your religious beliefs.	54	63	51

Statement	White	Black	Hispanic
When Jesus Christ lived on Earth, He committed sins, like other people.	50	43	7
The Bible provides absolute moral truths that are the same for all people in all situations, without exception.	47	66	47
It doesn't matter what religious faith you associate with because they all believe the same principles and truths.	47	45	52
People who do not consciously accept Jesus Christ as their Savior will be condemned to hell.	32	63	30
Most adult Christians are hypocrites.	32	36	33
The whole idea of sin is outdated.	28	19	30
The Bible does not provide many practical standards for living in today's world.	25	25	33
There are some crimes, sins or other behaviors people do that are so terrible that they cannot be forgiven by God.	21	11	28
God created humans, but He is no longer personally involved in your life or experiences.	13	7	20

ONE SIZE DOES NOT FIT ALL

Clearly, the three ethnic groups that dominate the teenaged population share many common dreams and perspectives, but they also have a sufficient number of unique qualities to distinguish each group in important ways. Treating all teenagers as if they have the same views, ideals and lifestyles makes little sense. Ministering to them in identical ways is just as foolish.

Notes

1. In this chapter I will emphasize the differences between white, black and Hispanic teens, but will not discuss the characteristics of Asian teens in the United States. This is solely because, at 4 percent of the teen population, our survey samples do

not provide us with a large enough base of Asian teens to reliably analyze and draw conclusions from. Our studies among Asian adults have shown that they are quite distinctive in their thought patterns, work habits, demographic profiles and life aspirations. It is my hope to someday soon have the funding to implement a large-scale study of the Asian-American population and how faith fits into their culture.

2. The information and lifestyle patterns noted in this section are drawn from our research but are consistent with a vast array of government studies. For more information on the characteristics of the various ethnic groups in the U.S., visit the federal government's general website for statistical studies at www.fedstats.gov. Among the studies that might be of greatest interest are *America's Children 1999*, the Census Bureau's series called *Facts for Features*, a regularly updated report entitled *Educational Attainment in the U.S.* and a series of reports frequently updated by the Census Bureau known as Current Population Reports.

3. The Barna Institute is a division of The Barna Research Group that conducts a variety of large-scale cooperative studies. The report on technology and faith, exploring the attitudes of national representative samples of teenagers, adults and Protestant pastors, is entitled *The Cyberchurch*. A previous study focused on the black population and resulted in a report entitled *African-Americans and Their Faith*. That report also evaluated the lifestyles, experiences and faith realities of black teens, black adults and the pastors of black churches. To purchase these reports, or learn more about what they contain, consult our website (www.barna.org).

CHAPTER 6

FAITH AND SPIRITUALITY

Faith is important to young people today. But just as James wrote that believing in God is not enough of a commitment—"even the demons believe that—and shudder" (Jas. 2:19)—neither is the fact that teenagers embrace spirituality as reason alone for celebration and high expectations.

Most teenagers think of themselves as Christians. For more than a decade, regardless of their beliefs and church attendance, more than four out of five teens have been describing their faith affiliation as Christian. Despite some minor fluctuations over the years, we find that things have changed little during the past decade. Currently, 86 percent describe themselves as Christian.

In spite of the infiltration of postmodern thinking and New Age practices, the virtual elimination of Christian activities and perspectives from public schools and the widespread exposure of teenagers to various faith groups, non-Christian religions are making minimal headway in their efforts to overtly attract young people. The Muslim and Buddhist faiths each claim about 1 percent of teens, as have the Jehovah's Witnesses. Hindus, Unitarians, Scientologists and Christian Scientists are each at less than one-half of 1 percent of the teen population. Jews have remained at about 2 percent of the teen universe, as have the Mormons. Even the faith positions that correlate most easily with post-modernism—i.e., atheism and agnosticism, have remained in the 7- to 10-percent range for the past several years.

There has been only the slightest in fluctuations regarding teens' denominational affiliations, too. The biggest transition has been a loss of adherents by the Catholic church, dropping from more than 30 percent adherence among self-described Christians in the early '90s—and as recently as 1997 and 1998—to just 22 percent in 2000. The mainline Protestant churches are standing still after a decade of slow decline, currently drawing about one of every five teens. Some of those losses have resulted in a small increase in the number of teens who have aligned themselves with charismatic and Pentecostal churches. However, only about 1 out of every 10 teens associates with such congregations. (There are tens of thousands more teens, by the way, who are practicing charismatics but attend a non-charismatic church. The charismatic gifts and demonstrations of spiritual power are a perfect fit with a generation that measures value on the basis of personal gain, dramatic experience and entertainment pizzazz.)

The major denominational affiliations have been static in recent years. Since the mid-'90s, Baptists have stayed in the 16- to 18-percent range, while other large denominations have shown a similar lack of growth (for instance, the Methodists at 7 percent, Lutherans at 5 percent and Presbyterians at 3 percent). Nondenominational churches have never really caught on with teens, attracting less than 2 percent of the teen body.

CHRISTIAN COMMITMENT

One way of evaluating people's dedication to Christianity is by asking those who call themselves Christian to describe how committed they are to that faith. Upon doing so, the results are disturbing: Only 3 out of every 10 self-described Christian teenagers claim to be "absolutely committed" to the Christian faith. The bulk of the teen universe is in the lukewarm category (half say they are "moderately committed"). Even when we focus on the born-again teens—the group whose relationship with Christ and understanding of His death and resurrection for their benefit should ignite passionate commitment—we find that only half of them (48 percent) claim to be absolutely devoted to the Christian faith.

The ambiguous commitment of most young "Christians"—two-thirds are "moderately," "not too" or "not at all" committed to their faith of choice—is a fitting reflection of the impact of a culture that is drifting toward postmodernism and in which spirituality is treated as just another consumer commodity, with one's choice of the day having no greater consequences than the brand of cereal purchased at the supermarket. Relatively few of these young people were merely providing a humble assessment of their inadequacy before the Lord. Rather, it seems evident that for the most part, they were being honest about the intensity of their commitment to Christianity.

COMMITMENT TO CHRISTIANITY
(base: self-described Christians)

	1997	1998	1999	2000
absolutely committed to it	29%	27%	26%	31%
moderately committed to it	47	53	57	49
not too committed to it	18	16	14	14
not at all committed to it	7	5	3	5
sample size	*620*	*605*	*614*	*605*

Throughout this book I have differentiated born-again teens from those who are not born again. In Barna Research surveys, a born-again

Christian is determined by asking two questions related to views about salvation. (The term "born again" is *not* used in the survey.) The first question posed is, "Have you ever made a personal commitment to Jesus Christ that is still important in your life today?" Those who answer in the affirmative are then asked a follow-up question, which provides respondents with seven options describing what they believe will happen to them after they die, and why. One of the options is "When I die I will go to heaven because I have confessed my sins and have accepted Jesus Christ as my Savior." Individuals who say that they have made a personal commitment to Jesus Christ that is still important in their life and who claim they know they will go to heaven because they have confessed their sins and accepted Jesus Christ as their Savior are categorized as born-again Christians. No one except God knows for sure, of course, but we have used this approach for two decades as a means of estimating the number of Christians in America and determining how that group differs from people who are not depending upon Christ alone for their eternal outcome.

Typically about 6 out of 10 teenagers say they have made a personal commitment to Christ. Among them, roughly 6 out of 10 believe they will have eternal salvation because of their confession of sins and acceptance of Jesus as their Savior. Therefore, the most current statistics show that one-third of the teen population (33 percent) is born again. That level has not varied in the past six years, although it does represent a marginal increase from the 28 percent measured in 1990.

Note, too, that among the people who call themselves Christians and claim to have made a personal commitment to Christ that is important in their lives, 4 out of 10 either believe their salvation is based on something other than grace (about 60 percent of those within this segment), or they do not know what will transpire after their death (the remaining 40 percent).

Barna Research has been tracking the "evangelical" population for two decades. An evangelical is someone defined by survey data in response to nine questions, all of which relate to beliefs. The scale requires a person to be born again; to describe religious faith as very important in his or her life; to affirm Jesus' sinless life; to believe in God as an omnipotent and omniscient deity who created the world and still rules the universe; to assert that the Bible is totally accurate in all that it teaches; to accept personal responsibility to evangelize; to believe that Satan exists; and to believe that salvation is possible by grace alone. This scale shows that just 4 percent of teenagers can be considered to be evangelicals. That is a far cry from the 10 percent measured in 1995. The current figure is just a few points lower than the national norm among adults (6 percent).

The decline in the number of evangelicals is a testimony to a pair of complementary national trends: the increase in biblical illiteracy and the move toward inclusive theology. The former behavioral pattern reflects people's disinterest in and declining involvement with the Bible. At the same time, we find a growing willingness among Americans to embrace all theology as equally valid, regardless of the genesis of the theology. The consequence is a watering down of Christian theology to such a low standard that it often conflicts with, rather than conforms to, Scripture.

WHAT TEENAGERS BELIEVE

Religious beliefs, regardless of their scriptural veracity, are an integral part of how teens view and cope with life. Four out of five teens say that their religious beliefs are very important in their life. But what do they believe?

Beliefs in God

Following in the footsteps of the adult population, more than 9 out of 10 teens—96 percent, to be precise—claim that they believe in God. But what is the nature of the God they embrace? Two-thirds of them believe in the God described in the Bible—the all-powerful, all-knowing, perfect creator of the universe who rules the world today. The remaining one-third is split between a variety of New Age, narcissistic and Eastern views of divinity. Eight percent believe that God refers to the total realization of personal, human potential, while a similar number contend that God represents a state of higher consciousness that a person may reach. Five percent believe in multiple gods, each of whom possesses different power and authority. Only a handful (4 percent) believes that every individual is a god, and just 4 percent state that there is no such thing or being as God. The remaining teens still have not come to a conclusion about the existence or nature of God.

Most teens (80 percent) believe that God created the universe. A similar percentage (84 percent) also believe that God is personally involved in people's lives; just one out of every seven says that after creating us He isolated Himself from human life and our daily experience. Yet, in spite of these orthodox views, two-thirds (63 percent) also believe that Muslims, Buddhists, Christians, Jews and all other people pray to the same god, even though they use different names for their god.

Beliefs About Jesus

Few teens doubt the existence of Jesus Christ. Nearly 9 out of 10 (87 percent) believe that Jesus Christ was a real person who lived on Earth. Almost 8 out of 10 (78 percent) believe that He was born to a virgin.

But more than half of all teenagers (53 percent) also believe that when He was on Earth Jesus committed sins. There is shockingly little difference between born-again and non-born-again teens on this matter: 4 out of 10 born-again teenagers contend that Jesus was a sinner.

The teaching of the Resurrection is muddled in the minds of many teens, too. Half of the teenaged population believes that Jesus was crucified and died, but that He did not return to life physically after the crucifixion.

Beliefs About the Holy Spirit

Most teenagers give verbal assent to the existence of the Trinity, although they do not really understand how it works or why it matters. This is perhaps best exemplified by the discovery that two-thirds of all teenagers (68 percent) say the Holy Spirit is a symbol of God's presence or power but is not a living entity. What is most amazing—and alarming—about this finding is that 64 percent of the born-again population accept this view, barely different than the 70 percent among the non-believing segment of teenagers. Blacks hold this view especially strongly (73 percent).

Beliefs About Satan

Satan has fooled millions of teenagers into soft-pedaling his existence. Two out of every three teenagers (65 percent) state that the devil is not a living being but is a symbol of evil. Even a majority of born-again teens (55 percent) has been seduced into accepting this view.

Beliefs About the Bible

As is true regarding so much of their faith, teenagers are confused about what to believe regarding the Bible. On the one hand, 6 out of 10 say that the Bible is totally accurate in all of its teachings. They perceive its content to be valid, too: 9 out of 10 teens deny that anyone who relies upon the Bible for moral guidance is foolish. They accept many of the fundamental teachings contained in the Scriptures. For instance, 3 out of 4 believe that all of the miracles described in the Bible actually took place. Seven out of 10 say that the notion of sin, originating in the Bible, is still a relevant concept for us today. In fact, 3 out of 4 teenagers suggest that the Bible provides us with many practical standards for contemporary life.

But teens' views of Scripture are corrupted in other ways. Three-quarters of them believe that a central message of the Bible is that God helps those who help themselves. As described earlier, there is ample confusion about whether or not the Bible provides insight into moral truth and, if it does, whether such truth is absolute or relative in nature. Nearly 6 out of 10 teens even agree that all religious faiths teach equally valid truths.

Beliefs About Evangelism and Salvation

The waters get very muddy when it comes to salvation. Consider the contradictions in what teenagers believe about eternity—not only contradictions of Scripture, but also inconsistencies within their own belief system.

Three out of 4 teenagers believe that God judges everyone after death. Six out of 10 say that forgiveness of sins is possible only through faith in Jesus Christ. Relatively few (21 percent) believe that there are some sins that we commit that not even God can forgive, or that people get reincarnated after they die (35 percent).

However, just one out of every three teens accepts the biblical teaching that people who do not consciously accept Jesus Christ as their Savior will be condemned to hell. Millions of teens have bought into a works-based theology, as exemplified by the three out of every five who believe that if a person is generally good, or does enough good things for others during their life, he or she will earn a place in heaven.

About half of all teenagers believe that they have a personal responsibility to tell other people their religious beliefs. Given what they actually believe, this may not be a behavior we want to encourage.

Amazingly, even though they have personally prayed to accept Jesus Christ as their Savior, half of all born-again teenagers believe that a person can earn his or her way into heaven. The evangelistic fervor of the body of believers is tempered by the fact that one-third (32 percent) reject the inevitability of condemnation for those who do not accept Jesus as their Savior.

Beliefs About Prayer

Most teenagers pray to God. A major impetus for such prayer is the belief held by more than four out of five teens (84 percent) that prayer can change what happens in life. This view is especially common among born agains (97 percent), blacks (98 percent) and girls (88 percent).

Beliefs About Spirituality

Just as millions of teenagers view eternal salvation by grace as an option to be chosen from a menu of viable routes to eternity with God, so do many teens look upon a life built upon spiritual clarity as just one of several reasonable alternatives. Two out of three teenagers endorse the notion that a person can lead a full and satisfying life even if they do not pursue spiritual development or maturity.

Beliefs About Angels

Teenagers accept the reality of spiritual beings. Four out of five (80 percent) believe that angels exist and influence people's lives. Although this is more likely to be accepted by girls (85 percent) than by boys (75 percent), even three-quarters of the non-Christian segment of teens believe in the existence and influence of angels.

Beliefs About the Role and Power of Faith

Faith is a powerful, if sometimes distorted, ingredient in the lives of teenagers. This goes beyond the view held by four-fifths of teenagers that their religious faith is very important in their lives. Seven out of 10 teens take it a step further and claim that the Christian faith is relevant to their lives today. The same proportion of teens admit that they can think of specific times recently when their religious beliefs actually changed the way they normally would have behaved. Two out of three even went so far as to say that they feel it is important for them to be members of a church. Whether or not they follow through on that commitment remains to be seen.

Beliefs About Faith in Jesus

It is one thing to call yourself a Christian, but something else to understand, share and model that faith. Some of the struggles that teenagers have in this regard are clearly demonstrated through the finding that half of the group says it does not matter what religious faith you associate with, because all of the major faith groups believe the same principles and truths. In addition, further confusion is evident in that one out of every four teens believes that what you do for other people is more important than what you believe about Jesus Christ.

WHAT TEENS BELIEVE

Statement	AST	ASW	DSW	DST
The Bible is totally accurate in all of its teachings.	40%	22%	22%	13%
You, personally, have a responsibility to tell other people your religious beliefs.	30	25	25	19
Your religious faith is very important in your life.	57	24	12	6
The devil, or Satan, is not a living being but is a symbol of evil.	34	31	13	19

Statement	AST	ASW	DSW	DST
If a person is generally good, or does enough good things for others during his or her life, he or she will earn a place in heaven.	34	27	13	25
When Jesus Christ lived on Earth He committed sins, like other people.	23	30	9	33
Muslims, Buddhists, Christians, Jews and all other people pray to the same god, even though they use different names for their god.	30	33	14	20***
Prayer can change what happens in life.	52	32	8	6***
Jesus Christ was a real person.	70	17	3	4***
A person can lead a full and satisfying life even if he or she does not pursue spiritual development or maturity.	26	39	17	16***
People who do not consciously accept Jesus Christ as their Savior will be condemned to hell.	23	12	27	36***
Forgiveness of sins is only possible through faith in Jesus Christ.	41	20	19	17***
Angels exist and influence people's lives.	46	34	10	7***
The universe was originally created by God.	64	16	11	7***
All people will be judged by God after they die, regardless of their religious beliefs.	56	17	15	11***
Jesus Christ was born to a virgin.	61	17	11	8***
All of the miracles described in the Bible actually took place.	52	24	13	10***
The whole idea of sin is outdated.	7	19	25	45***
All religious faiths teach equally valid truths.	21	37	20	19***
After death, people are reincarnated—that is, they return to Earth in another life form.	13	22	22	41***
The Holy Spirit is a symbol of God's presence or power but is not a living entity.	36	32	14	15*
After He was crucified and died, Jesus Christ did not return to life physically.	27	24	16	30*

Statement	AST	ASW	DSW	DST
Your religious beliefs actually change the way you behave.	46	27	16	11**
God created humans, but He is no longer personally involved in your life or experiences.	5	9	18	66**
There are some crimes, sins or other behaviors people do that are so terrible that they cannot be forgiven by God.	10	11	18	59**
It doesn't matter what religious faith you associate with because they all believe the same principles and truths.	20	28	22	29**

Key: AST=agree strongly; ASW=agree somewhat; DSW=disagree somewhat; DST=disagree strongly.

Notes: * indicates this information is from the national study of teenagers conducted in 1997, N=620; ** indicates this information is from the national study of teens conducted in 1998, N=605; *** indicates this information is from the national study of teens conducted in 1999, N=614. All other data are from our national study of 605 teenagers in 2000. Percentages may not add up to 100 percent due to exclusion of those who said "don't know."

The encouraging news is that as teens struggle with their faith, whatever it may be, their experience may well lead them to some positive conclusions. Three-quarters of them stated that their religious beliefs have actually changed their behavior in the past. Recognizing the power of faith to guide and to change them is a laudable step toward genuine spiritual insight and growth. On the other hand, we have reason to worry about the capacity of teens to change their minds about the things they presently believe. Two-thirds claim that they are very familiar with all of the major principles and teachings of the Christian faith. Worse, three-fourths of all teens contend that they are not likely to change what they believe in the future.

OTHER RELIGIOUS BELIEFS OF TEENAGERS

Statement	Agree	Disagree
Your religious beliefs are not likely to change in the future.	73%	25%*
The Christian faith is relevant to your life today.	71	26
You can think of specific times recently when your religious beliefs actually changed the way you normally would have behaved.	69	29
You are very familiar with all of the major principles and teachings of the Christian faith.	66	31*
You feel it is important for you to be a member of a church.	66	33
The Bible provides a clear and totally accurate description of moral truth.	61	34
The Bible provides absolute moral truths that are the same for all people in all situations, without exception.	49	49
What you do for other people is more important than what you believe about Jesus Christ.	25	66
The Bible does not provide many practical standards for living in today's world.	23	74
Anyone who relies upon the Bible for moral guidance is foolish.	7	91

Notes: * percentages may not add up to 100 percent due to exclusion of those who said "don't know." ** indicates this information is from the national study of teens conducted in 2000, N=605. All other data are from our national study of 614 teenagers in 1999.

WHAT BORN-AGAIN TEENS BELIEVE

If all of this seems somewhat discouraging, don't give up hope! Here's some good news: Born-again teens do have a somewhat different belief profile from that of their non-born-again peers. As the figures in the following table show, in most instances there is a 20-percentage-point difference or more between the two groups.

Then again, we have to recognize that there is a lot of garbage that passes for spiritual insight among young believers. For instance, we have to address the fact that half of all believers say that good people can earn their salvation, or that 4 out of 10 argue that Jesus committed sins, or that a majority say there is no such thing as Satan. What we believe matters. Our beliefs affect our worldview, our relationships, our choices and our behavior. How sad it is when well-intentioned believers make inappropriate choices on the basis of their beliefs—because their beliefs, unbeknownst to them, are not biblical. Such ignorance has even more disastrous effects because Christians share the faith that they believe. When a Christian shares lies in the name of truth, misleading others in the process, a harvest of deception and misfortune is unwittingly sown, negatively affecting the lives of many.

A COMPARISON OF THE BELIEFS OF BORN-AGAIN TEENS AND NON-BORN-AGAIN TEENS

Statement	Born Again		Not Born Again	
	AGR	DIS	AGR	DIS
The Bible is totally accurate in all of its teachings.	86%	13%	50%	47%
You, personally, have a responsibility to tell other people your religious beliefs.	79	21	44	55
The devil, or Satan, is not a living being but is a symbol of evil.	55	41	68	27
If a person is generally good, or does enough good things for others during his or her life, he or she will earn a place in heaven.	48	52	67	31
When Jesus Christ lived on Earth, He committed sins, like other people.	40	58	60	34
Muslims, Buddhists, Christians, Jews and all other people pray to the same god, even though they use different names for their god.	42	52	72	26*
Prayer can change what happens in life.	97	3	77	19*
Jesus Christ was a real person.	90	6	86	8*

Statement	Born Again		Not Born Again	
	AGR	DIS	AGR	DIS
A person can lead a full and satisfying life even if he or she does not pursue spiritual development or maturity.	44	55	73	24*
People who do not consciously accept Jesus Christ as their Savior will be condemned to hell.	67	32	22	76*
Forgiveness of sins is only possible through faith in Jesus Christ.	88	12	50	47*
All people will be judged by God after they die, regardless of their religious belief.	91	8	61	37*
All of the miracles described in the Bible actually took place.	95	5	63	34*
All religious faiths teach equally valid truths.	53	45	61	36*
After death, people are reincarnated—that is, they return to Earth in another life form.	17	82	46	50*

Key: AGR = agree; DIS = disagree.

Notes: * indicates this information is from a Barna Research Group national study of 614 teenagers conducted in 1999. All other data are from a national study of 605 teenagers conducted by Barna Research in 2000. Percentages may not add up to 100 percent due to the exclusion of those who said "don't know."

RELIGIOUS BEHAVIOR

While youth ministry has become a standard ministry program in tens of thousands of churches, and parachurch ministries geared to serving and developing youth have become a mainstay of the ministry environment, there has been surprisingly little growth in the involvement of teenagers in the life of the Church over the past decade.

As the figures in the following table show, slightly more than half of all teens who describe themselves as Christian or who attend a Christian church are present in the worship services of their church on a typical weekend. One out of three teens reads from the Bible during a typical week, excluding when they are at a church service or event. About the same proportion attends youth-group activities at the church during a typical week, and roughly the same percentage is involved in a Sunday School class in a typical weekend. There have been minor fluctuations in these statistics throughout the course of the decade, but the end result as we finish the decade is that these figures have not changed in 10 years.

Information that we have begun collecting more recently suggests that in addition to the activities described earlier, about 3 out of 10 teens are active in a small group, and more than 8 out of 10 pray during the course of a week.

RELIGIOUS ACTIVITY IN THE PAST SEVEN DAYS
(base: self-described Christians or attend a Christian church)

Activity	1990	1997	1998	1999	2000
attend a church service, not including a special event such as a wedding or funeral	54%	52%	53%	56%	52%
read from the Bible (excluding while at a church)	33	34	33	35	36
attend a church youth group activity or event, other than a small group or Sunday School class	29	37	35	32	36
attend a Sunday School class at a church	NA	35	39	35	40
participate in a small group that meets regularly for Bible study, prayer or Christian fellowship, not including a Sunday School or 12-step group	NA	30	27	29	28
pray to God	NA	81	80	89	84

In addition, two-thirds of born-again teenagers said that within the past 12 months they had explained their religious beliefs to someone who had different beliefs, in the hope that they might accept Jesus Christ as their Savior. A surprisingly large percentage of self-identified Christians who are not born again also shared their faith with others during that time frame (34 percent). These figures have remained the same over the past four years.

The most striking realization to emerge from all of these faith participation statistics is that teenagers have higher levels of participation in organized religious activity than do adults. While the surveys indicate that parents mandate some of this involvement, a large majority of teens engages in such activity out of personal choice rather than in response to parental pressure. Much of that personal interest is keenly tied to the involvement of the individual's peer group: Where the group goes, so go its individuals.

A COMPARISON OF THE RELIGIOUS ACTIVITY OF ADULTS AND TEENAGERS, IN A TYPICAL WEEK
(base: attend a Christian church)

Activity	Teens	Adults
prayed to God	84%	89%
attended a church service, not including a special event such as a wedding or funeral	52	47
read from the Bible (excluding while at a church)	36	45
attended a Sunday School class at a church	40	21
participated in a small group that meets regularly for Bible study, prayer or Christian fellowship, not including a Sunday School or 12-step group	28	18
donated money to a church	40	61

A study among teenagers that we conducted in 2000 for the Texas-based ministry Wisdom Works found that teenagers are very open with their peers regarding their personal faith beliefs and practices. Not only do three out of every four teens discuss their religious views with peers during a typical quarter, but half of all non-Christian youths described themselves as "open to spirituality" and supported that claim by entertaining frequent discussions about faith matters with friends.

Even though our research emphasizes that there are relatively few evangelicals among the nation's teenagers, there are many who share their faith in Christ with nonbelievers. The Wisdom Works study identified about one-third of all teens as "evangelizers"—i.e., individuals who share their faith in Christ with someone in the hope of the nonbeliever's embracing Christ as his or her Savior. In fact, among the Christian evan-gelizers half had prayed for the salvation of specific friends or family members. The study further showed that the inadequate witness of those well-intentioned believers, their inadequate knowledge of the Christian faith, and their lack of preparation for evangelistic encounters often blunt their evangelistic efforts.[1]

INVOLVEMENT IN A CHURCH YOUTH GROUP

About two-thirds of all teenagers have some interaction with a church youth program during the course of a typical month. That means that of the 22 million teens in the nation, nearly 15 million of them have some exposure to Christianity through youth groups. A significant, if minority, portion of that number is comprised of individuals who do not consider themselves to be Christian, and another significant share is made up of people who call themselves Christian but are not born again. The data show that half of the kids who call themselves Christian and participate in youth groups in a typical month are not born again—a pool of more than 7 million unsaved kids who journey to the church on a regular basis.

What do they like best about the youth group experience? Half of them listed the presence of their friends, making personal relationships three times the attraction of any other factor listed. Other important ele-ments included the opportunity to learn about God and the Christian faith (mentioned by one out of four) and the activities and events that take place (listed by one out of five). Relatively few teens mentioned the charisma of the youth leader, the music or the opportunity to experience God's presence.

When pressed to identify the single most important reason why they attend a youth group, the picture changes significantly. It turns out that relationships bring the kids to the place, but they will not return unless the church delivers the goods. What are they looking for? Substance. Learning practical and credible insights about God was listed twice as often as anything else as the most important reason for returning. The fellowship, the games, the music, the casual and friendly atmosphere—all of those elements are important to getting kids in the door—the first time. Getting them there on subsequent occasions requires those benefits plus solid, personally applicable content.

Why doesn't music alone attract them? Because they can usually see better music elsewhere and in a more conducive environment. Why don't games serve as a sufficient allure? Because they can play games in many places—and usually have greater control over the nature and conduct of those experiences. Why won't they come if a lot of kids their own age are present? Because it's the presence of their "tribe," not the mere presence of people from their generation, that makes the experience worthwhile to them.

FUTURE CHURCH ATTENDANCE

While there is much activity on church campuses today among teenagers (as will be described in the pages that follow), the future of church attendance is on shaky ground according to the very teens who are currently so actively involved in church-related endeavors.

One unmistakable indication of the brewing trouble comes from the response to a question concerning how likely teens say they are to attend church once they are independent. After they graduate from high school or move away from home, just two out of five teens contend it is "very likely" that they will attend a Christian church on a regular basis, and another two out of five say it is "somewhat likely." What makes these figures most alarming is that questions of this type typically produce an overestimate of future behavior. If we apply a "correction factor" to these responses, we would estimate that about one out of three teenagers is likely to actually attend a Christian church after they leave home.[2] To place that in context, twice as many adults currently attend church activities. If this estimate is even close to accurate, it is a harbinger of difficult days for the Church. A drop of 50 percent in potential attendees would have a calamitous effect on the American Church.

One of the associated trends that must also be taken into account is that when teenagers do attend a church, they do not always attend the same one. They are very comfortable church hopping, especially when it involves attending in the company of their friends. Only half of the teens who presently attend Christian churches say that they always attend the same church every time they attend a church service or event. Almost as many say they usually attend the same church but occasionally go to other churches, and another 6 percent typically divide their attendance among two or more different churches that they like. This latter tendency is less pronounced among teens than among adults, but a major reason is because of their limited mobility.

Teenagers are quite open to visiting new churches and having a variety of religious experiences. Given their philosophical inclinations—e.g., all churches teach the same basic lessons, there is no absolute moral truth, faith is important but church loyalty is not, and so forth—we can expect multiple church homes to become even more common than is the case today. In fact, among teens who presently attend a Christian church, half admit that they would be likely to visit some other Christian church if they were invited to do so. When they were asked which of several marketing efforts would be most effective at attracting them to the church, a personal invitation from a friend was the winner, hands down. Nine out of 10 teenagers said they would attend because of the personal invitation, compared to just 4 percent responding to a special event (such as a concert) and less than one-half of 1 percent attending in response to a brochure received in the mail.

Their loyalty is not to an institution or a faith perspective but to the people whom they trust. When their "tribe" journeys to a particular faith center, individuals in that group are more inclined to attend because of the existing relationships than because of the reputation, programs or events of the church. Don't relax because of the large percentage of teenagers who are presently engaged in the life of the Church. They are not coming for the reasons we might desire—and we have little chance of them coming in the future unless we consistently satisfy their deepest spiritual and personal needs.

WHAT MAKES A CHURCH APPEALING?

The importance of church life in the spiritual development of people cannot be overestimated—nor should it be minimized. But we also know that teenagers are still in a formative stage spiritually. They attend churches for a variety of reasons—and those experiences will shape their desires and expectations regarding church life as they age. What matters to them as they explore church life?

We asked a national sample of teens to imagine having just moved to a different state and decided to look for a church to attend. What key factors would determine whether or not they would return to a church they had visited? (We asked this question only among teens who described themselves as Christians or among non-Christians who were open to attending a Christian church in the future.)

The answers ranged far and wide. The most common reply, listed by one-third of the young adults, was that they wanted a church where the attitude and demeanor of the people was positive, welcoming and upbeat. The importance of the overall feel of the church environment—the ministry ambiance—was mentioned by one out of every seven teenagers. Overall, then, almost half of the respondents cited some dimension of the ministry atmosphere as the most crucial element in their selection.

The next most prolific category of responses related to the community developed among the people. Teens identified this by listing concerns such as a desire for genuine relationships, a focus on creating real community, the hope of being with people who were serious about their faith and about each other, wanting to belong to a place that was family-oriented and seeking a congregation in which the people truly supported each other. Just over one-quarter of the teens interviewed listed such requirements.

The third-highest expression of interest related to receiving high-quality teaching and preaching. This, too, was named by roughly one-quarter of the teens. This was loosely associated with another significant need, that of associating with a church that had appropriate and helpful beliefs. The theological tendencies of the church was named by one out of every eight teenagers.

Other desirable church attributes mentioned by 5 percent to 10 percent of the teens included the character and qualities of the pastor; the nature and quality of the music; the quality of the church's programs, especially the youth ministry; the denominational affiliation of the church (usually listed by Catholics); and the size of the church (divided evenly between having a small and large church). Less frequently listed factors included the demographics of the congregation, the location of the church, the nature of its facilities and the outreach efforts of the body.

To get a more refined understanding of the importance of various factors, we then asked the same group to react to each of 18 factors that might be included in their deliberations. The findings are generally consistent with their previous statements about what is important to them but provide additional contours to their dream church.

As expected, the top-rated factors pertained to the people. The friendliness of the people and how much they care about each other were identified as powerful determinants in their assessment of the attraction of a church. Three out of every four teens deemed these elements to be very important.

The next most important factors were the sermon quality and the theological beliefs or doctrine of the church. Two-thirds of all teens listed each of these as critical factors. Not far behind was the importance of the church being consistently involved in helping poor and disadvantaged people. Our past research has shown that this is used by people as a practical measure of the heart of the church. Being connected to a group that serves people in need is very appealing to people of all ages—but especially to young people.

About half of all teens indicated that liking the pastor was very important to them. Try as we might to avoid building personality-driven churches, the fact remains that the charisma of the primary minister makes a big difference in many people's willingness to associate with a church. That individual often embodies the personality of the church; how well visitors connect with that persona affects their likelihood of returning. The other factor that made a big difference to half of the respondents was the quality of the ministry to children.

The convenience of the worship service times was a major factor for about one-third, while slightly fewer listed the quality of the adult Sunday School classes as a major consideration. One out of four teens held each of four factors to be of substantial importance: the quality and the amount of music in the worship services, how many people their own age attend the church and how many of their personal friends attend the church.

About one out of every five teens cited the importance of the type of music in the services, and how many different types of ministries and programs exist beyond the weekend services. The least importance was assigned to the distance of the church from their home, the length of the sermons, and the availability of midweek small groups or home groups in which they could participate.

WHAT TEENAGERS MAY LOOK FOR IN A CHURCH IN THE FUTURE
(N=614)

Factor	How Important Is This Factor?		
	Very	Somewhat	Not Too
how friendly the people in the church are to visitors	76%	20%	4%
how much the people seem to care about each other	76	20	4
the quality of the sermons that are preached	66	27	7
the theological beliefs and doctrine of the church	64	27	7
how much the church is involved in helping poor and disadvantaged people	62	34	4
how much you like the pastor	52	33	14
the quality of the programs and classes for children	49	34	17
having convenient service times	37	43	20
the quality of the adult Sunday School classes	30	43	27
the quality of the music in the service	27	46	27
how many people your age attend the church	26	49	23
the amount of music included in the service	24	40	36
how many good friends you know who attend that church	24	42	35
the type of music in the weekend service	22	40	37

Factor	How Important Is This Factor?		
	Very	Somewhat	Not Too
how many different types of ministries and other programs they have besides the weekend services	22	53	24
how far the church is located from your home	18	43	33
the length of the sermons	17	48	35
the availability of midweek small groups or home groups to join	16	49	34

The needs of teens who describe themselves as Christian are notably divergent from the needs of non-Christians who might attend a church if invited. A comparison of the needs of each group are shown in the following table. The self-identified Christians are much more likely to care about the quality of the sermons, the content of the church's beliefs, how much they like the pastor and the quality of the adult Sunday School classes. They are also somewhat more interested in the availability of small-group opportunities, although relatively few teenagers, Christian or not, expressed much interest in small groups.

WHAT TEENAGERS MAY LOOK FOR IN A CHURCH IN THE FUTURE
(N=614)

Factor	Self-Identified Christian?		
	All Teens	Yes	No
how friendly the people in the church are to visitors	76%	78%	66%
how much the people seem to care about each other	76	76	76
the quality of the sermons that are preached	66	69	43
the theological beliefs and doctrine of the church	64	66	47
how much the church is involved in helping poor and disadvantaged people	62	62	57
how much you like the pastor	52	54	31

Factor	All Teens	Self-Identified Christian? Yes	No
the quality of the programs and classes for children	49	49	50
having convenient service times	37	36	45
the quality of the adult Sunday School classes	30	32	17
the quality of the music in the service	27	27	25
how many people your age attend the church	26	27	35
the amount of music included in the service	24	23	28
how many good friends you know who attend that church	24	22	35
the type of music in the weekend service	22	22	22
how many different types of ministries and other programs they have besides the weekend services	22	23	18
how far the church is located from your home	18	17	27
the length of the sermons	17	17	12
the availability of midweek small groups or home groups to join	16	17	5

Those who did not identify themselves as Christians showed more interest in factors such as how many of their friends are attending the church and the nearness of the church to their home. If we rank the 18 factors in descending order of importance to this group, the data show that these potential attendees have a very different set of priorities than do the self-described Christians. The elements that earn a higher ranking among the nonbelievers include having a congregation that is truly caring, a church that serves the poor, the presence of good children's ministries, convenience and having friends in the congregation.

Again, the obvious outcome is that while content matters, to those who are outside of the church the substance offered by the church is less important than how the experience feels. Outsiders are not willing to go too far out of their way to have that experience, since they are not yet convinced that the product will justify the investment. Realize that the typical non-attendee's mind is already made up regarding church. If we hope to persuade them to try a church experience we must surround them with friends who are warm and authentically caring, who invite them to visit, and then help those who need help the most (the needy and children). They do not come for music or preaching; they come for an experience that is made whole by the presence of people they know, trust and can take their cues from.

These insights provide us with a good starting point for building ministries that will attract teenagers once they are independent and making their own decisions about whether or not to attend a church and which one to attend. There are no "can't miss" marketing campaigns, no fail-safe ministry programs and no guarantees they will give a church—or any church—a fair shot. But the more we listen to their hearts and respond according to their expressed needs, the better are the chances that we may avoid a mass exodus of young people from the family of God.

Notes

1. The findings from the study we conducted for Wisdom Works are available to interested ministries. The study examined the evangelistic activity of teenagers and how their impact might be enhanced and expanded. Further information about the study can be obtained from our website, www.barna.org, in relation to the report entitled *Teenagers and Evangelism*.
2. This correction factor is based upon a variety of studies we have conducted in which we asked people to estimate a future behavior, then determined the percentage of people who followed through in the manner they had predicted.

CHAPTER 7

CHALLENGES ON THE ROAD LESS TRAVELED

One of the most consistent revelations from our research over the years has been that parents and young people have one important view in common: Most parents say they love their kids but are ecstatic that they no longer parent a teenager, and most adults under the age of 40 say they would not want to go through their teenaged years again. It seems that no matter how you slice it, the teen years are challenging and difficult—and becoming more so all the time. Many survive those years, but few pray for a time warp that would leave them permanently ensconced in those turbulent years.

Unless Christ returns in the near future, however, millions of parents, teenagers and youth leaders will experience those years from their respective angles, for better or worse. What can we learn from the research that may improve the experience for all involved?

A Few Words for Parents

Teenagers crave the mind and heart of their parents, but it all starts with a parent's willingness to listen. For a dozen years or more the young listened to their parents; once they reach high school, most young people figure it's their turn to be heard. But what should parents be listening for?

One approach would be to build such an environment and relationship of trust that the young person feels comfortable sharing significant information about his or her life. When they do so, they are essentially leaving clues for the observant parent to follow up on. Here are a few of the more important clues to be watching out for.

The Search for Meaning

Most young adults go through a search for significance, seeking to discern meaning, purpose and truth in life. Because their cultural context has made life incredibly complex and has removed most of the anchors and guideposts that formerly made sense of reality, teenagers are in a highly experimental mode and want exposure to as many viable options as may exist.

Parents cannot force a worldview or philosophy of life upon young individuals, but they can provide key insights and connections that will help them see life from a different vantage point or understand a dimension of life more thoroughly and accurately. The means to such an end would be to encourage the teenager to constantly communicate what he or she is thinking and feeling; to tease out the true meaning of what is being said and the issues with which the teen is grappling; to engage the teen in conversation, offering a few morsels of wisdom along with a battery of clarifying, non-threatening questions for him or her to consider; and providing him or her with encouragement and reinforcement when he or she appears to make progress.

Define Appropriate Values

Values describe what is meaningful, appropriate and worthwhile in life. As teens strive to define who they are and what matters in life, their values will be the core around which such matters are determined. Because Americans are not very reflective but are more inclined to be reactive, what is modeled for them takes root; we tend to imitate rather than create. The values that organize our lives and make sense of our situations are a powerful influence on the character we embrace and the lifestyle we pursue. Parents who have thought through and who live in accordance with a consistent and Christian value set have a much greater chance of seeing those values absorbed by their children than do parents who leave it to chance and hope for the best. Discussing these choices is only one element in the process; demonstrating what they look like, in practice, is the most powerful influence.

Family Connection

Most teens want to feel as if they are part of a family that knows them, loves them and will look out for them. Often, they express these needs in ways that appear to reject family, but the deeper need exists nevertheless. Parents must provide focused leadership to family members; have a vision for what kind of family they want to have and the strategies it will take to facilitate such a family experience; make a commitment to the sacrifices it will take to achieve their vision; and consistently follow through on their vision.

A healthy family experience is one that addresses the central dimensions of the teens' life with sensitivity and wisdom.

Providing young people with outlets for their physical development, emotional growth, spiritual maturation and intellectual curiosity are important. We cannot expect teens to listen to advice or take our challenges seriously unless they believe that we have their best interests in mind, have confidence in our judgment, experience times when we struggle through issues and situations alongside of them, give ample evidence of how our lives are completely affected by what we believe and how we interact with God and our faith principles, and watch us maintain an unending commitment to learning and growing.

In a study we conducted several years ago, one of the most powerful lessons we gained was that a huge gift to children is for their parents to remain married. Adults have many justifications for dissolving a troubled marriage, but apart from situations in which abuse is involved, the long-term positive effect of a husband and wife staying together through the myriad joys and conflicts of marriage sends a compelling message to young people about commitment, loyalty, love and sacrifice. Perhaps more than anything else we studied, staying married provides kids with a permanent, treasured gift.

Faith Connection

Kids—even teenagers—take cues from their parents. Our research typically shows that when parents are absolutely committed to their faith and live consistently according to their faith views and values, kids are much more likely to accept what has been modeled for them as reasonable, without it being jammed down their throats. The keys to successfully passing on faith from one generation to another relate to making faith central to one's existence, avoiding lifestyle hypocrisy and integrating faith behaviors and values into everything the family does as a unit and as individuals.

Teenagers rarely embrace Christianity if their family has treated faith as a Sunday-morning experience; it must be the focal point of their lives. The family must not only attend church services together but must also discuss their beliefs, interpret opportunities and experiences through a faith filter, and treat each other as spiritual beings who share a connection through Christ. In practical terms, the family—as a family unit—must also have worship experiences, pray together about significant personal needs, study the meaning of Scriptures together and serve others. Pragmatic expressions of faith—such as forgiveness, encouragement and kindness—also make a deep impression on the hearts and minds of young people. In other words, if we want children—even teenagers—to imitate the life of Christ, we have to pave the way by doing so for them.

A FEW WORDS FOR YOUTH WORKERS

Having worked with and studied the ministries of many effective youth workers across the nation, I'd like to offer a few observations about what seems to give those servants significant impact in the lives of young people. I offer these insights with some hesitation, since these notations are based upon subjective interpretations drawn from my interaction with thousands of churches and numerous youth ministries across the nation. Treat them as suggestions for consideration rather than irrefutable laws for success.

Effective youth workers seem to prepare differently, and then they perform their ministries on the basis of several key activities. Let me first describe a handful of key equipping practices and then note the ways in which they minister that seem to have positive outcomes.

Preparation for Effective Ministry to Teens

Understand the World of the Teenager

To gain the trust and respect of teens, and to have an impact upon them, effective youth workers make a concerted effort to inhabit the world of the teenager. Often, youth workers who mean well but have limited influence are disabled in their ministry by expecting teens to abandon what comes naturally in favor of entering the adult world. These youth workers push kids to think and act like short adults. In contrast, the most effective youth workers encourage young people to be young—acting and thinking like a human being in process. These ministers accept the immaturity and the impulsiveness as a natural aspect of being young—an aspect that may never be enjoyed at any other stage in these young people's lives; so they ought to exploit it and enjoy it while they can.

But this is more than just letting kids be kids. To be effective, the youth worker must comprehend the cultural context of the young person. That requires exploring what life is like for young people (e.g., reading their magazines, watching some of their favorite TV shows and movies, talking to them about their experiences and challenges). It demands constant reinterpretation of events and experiences to perceive the meaning of life through the eyes of a teenager. To provide contextual wisdom and practical advice, a youth leader must retain a balance of biblical values and cultural sensitivity—with the dominant culture of concern being that of the young person, not the adult.

Enter with a Worldview

One of the tragedies of youth ministries across the nation is that both professional and laypeople who minister to teenagers last for a short period of time. A primary reason is that teens always push the limits and test the mettle of their seniors. A youth worker who enters with good intentions but without a predetermined worldview will be immobilized by the tornado of challenging questions, activities and ideas of teens.

Effective youth workers have worked hard for many years to understand their faith and how it best becomes integrated into the practical situations of life. Because behavioral modeling is one of the keys to influencing teens, such modeling is unlikely to be consistent and biblical unless the youth worker has paid the dues to develop such a life perspective. When they have mastered this process, their leadership and influence are a natural extension of who they are rather than a series of learned or imitated behaviors based upon training for youth work.

Enter with a Philosophy of Youth Ministry

In like manner, we also discovered that the youth workers who affect the most lives do so partially because they have carefully and painstakingly thought through their philosophy of human development, the nature of the youth subculture, the role of Christianity in a young person's life, and the place of the youth worker and his or her ministry efforts in the young person's growth process. Too often we have observed well-intentioned individuals who had some training in youth ministry who were eaten alive by teens who sensed a weak link in the ministry chain: a schooled youth worker who was not authentically interacting with the youth subculture on the basis of a deeper and more fundamental perspective about the purpose of his or her involvement. "Warm bodies" and "volunteers" don't last long in outreach to teens. The staff and laity who outlast teens—and do so with outstanding results—have a clear vision of why they are engaged in youth work, how their efforts fit into a continuum of moral and spiritual development in a young person's life and how to evaluate the influence they are having in the individual's life.

Pray Daily

Effective youth workers pray for the development of each of the teenagers with whom they are interacting. Importantly, those prayers are not the occasional, spontaneous, generic requests for progress and impact that typify the efforts of youth workers. Their prayers have three elements. First, they identify each teen by name. Second, they address the particular needs of each individual in the youth group. Third, the youth worker intercedes on behalf of each young person every day.

One of the implications of this process, then, is that the youth worker must know his or her young charges rather well. This means regular communication and attentive listening, as well as consistent follow-through to stay current on conditions in the teens' lives. As much as anything else, when a young person knows that someone is praying—seriously and consistently—for them, they feel a unique bond and a sense of being cared for that is difficult to replicate in other ways. This alone opens many doors for personal ministry.

Find Resources

Youth workers who make a difference have no hesitation to go to bat for the needs of their youth group. They call in favors from friends, seek resources from the church that might not seem to be available and develop creative solutions to problems that might otherwise hinder the ministry's efficacy. These same individuals would blush at the aggressiveness or brashness they exhibit in pursuing resources to further their youth work if they were to use the same methods in other walks of their lives. However, driven to help kids and unwilling to let a mere absence of material goods or relational connections stand in the way of transforming young lives, these leaders do what it takes to maximize their impact for the Kingdom in the lives of kids. Their mind-set is that the resources exist—they simply have not been accumulated in the appropriate manner for their ultimate purpose.

Performance of Ministry Duties

Intimate Involvement

Observing the work of these leaders is fascinating because you clearly see that it is not so much about telling teens what to do as it is about being their friend and helping them through tough or challenging moments. The quality of interaction that is the norm between effective youth workers and teenagers rivals that of a good parent and his or her child. Ultimately, these youth workers care about the teens to whom they are ministering—and their depth of caring is provided at a level that cannot be faked, nor can the teens overlook the significant commitment that has been made to them.

This type of involvement is based upon vulnerability. The youth workers I've watched made it work because they were willing to shed their protective armor and be real with teens. This requires a commitment of time to get to know the teen, to share experiences and to create a deeper relationship. But this ministry also demands a level of transparency that would scare off all but the most committed servants. Admitting mistakes or lack of understanding are important ingredients in such relationships.

This involvement is also based on a willingness to stand beside young people when they are going through their darkest hours. Calling them during their times of travail, hanging out with them at times other than during designated ministry times, and sending them e-mails or postcards to certify their understanding and concern cements the relationship and the trust the youth worker needs in order to have a lasting impact. I have to admit that I was shocked to find that many of these youth workers were closer to these kids than the teens' own parents were—and, in many cases, were relied upon more than the parent during times of stress or crisis. Obviously, there is a fine line to be walked between supporting a parent and replacing a parent, but a levelheaded youth worker can make that distinction—and add huge value to the life of a young person in so doing.

Modeling

Teenagers have a very sensitive hypocrisy meter—especially among the do-gooders at church who want to remold them into different people. What does it take to crash through the defenses and the skepticism of the young adult? A lifestyle that matches the teaching provided by the adults. It is the consistency of thought, word and deed in the life of the youth workers that gain them the respect of teens. It doesn't matter how many books these individuals have read (or written), what degrees they possess or how esteemed they are in the adult world. The bottom line is that until youth workers live the lessons they preach, their words fall on deaf ears.

Experiential Learning

The most effective way to teach young people is to engage them in the process. Talking at them may work well if our objective is memorization and regurgitation, but experience has amply demonstrated that teens absorb principles and values best when they have the chance to participate in developing a deeply-rooted comprehension and application of those elements.

Great youth workers emphasize interactive, hands-on learning experiences. Preaching at kids has surprisingly little effect; working alongside of them to enable them to live the lessons of Scripture changes their lives.

Unapologetic Commitment

Often I am astounded at the great lengths our churches go to in order to provide teens with a fun, fast-paced experience that virtually masks the underlying reasons for the experience. The most effective youth workers I have studied take a different tact: extreme honesty. They makes no bones about the fact that the reason for the group being together is to move them to know, love and serve Jesus Christ, and that success in the ministry is about the lives of teens being transformed into Christ's likeness. These individuals are sensitive, caring, loving, committed, superb role models—but they are also incredibly up-front and unwavering about what motivates them to give up their time and energy for teens. Again, this truthfulness builds respect and trust.

A Few Words for Church Leaders

Our work with young people also lends itself to a few general comments about ministering to teens. Allow me to provide a few additional insights gleaned from studying churches that impact teenagers in ways that transcend the norm.

I am convinced that we sometimes blur the distinction between what we have to do to attract teens to the church (i.e., marketing) and what we must do to impact them for Christ (i.e., ministry). Too often, it seems, we surrender ministry value for marketing impact—that is, we give up the responsibility to facilitate life change in order to succeed at attracting a crowd.

How do we do this? By performing music, dramas and offering amusing teaching rather than engaging them in authentic worship and serious discipleship. By striving to facilitate relationships rather than providing them with accountability. By taking the easy way out and teaching for factual recall rather than for character development. By bringing the ministry to them instead of inviting them to grow by ministering to others.

We have mastered the art of drawing a crowd, but at the expense of drilling deep into lives of teenagers with spiritual truths. Games, loud music, interactive discussions, silly skits—all of those means have a place in youth ministry, but they must have a meaningful connection to the ultimate purpose of the ministry. If those approaches are justified sole-ly because they help us to recruit a larger number of young people, then we will win the battle but lose the war. We must remain focused on the larger mission and vision that God entrusts to His leaders for why we strive to influence the lives of young people.

One of the skills sadly absent from so many youth ministries and churches these days is that of conversation. Perhaps because Americans are so busy and so achievement oriented, we don't take time to have protracted dialogues; this is the age of the sound bite. Sound-bite Christianity has fostered the deterioration of the Church, and it is undermining the depth of knowledge, character and faith of young peo-ple, too. Several years ago I noted that the most effective form of sharing Christ among young people was Socratic evangelism—a process that takes time, relationship, conversation and a deep understanding of one's own faith principles.[1] Sadly, many youth ministries persist in reliance upon antiquated, linear approaches to making Christ and the Christian faith real to teenagers.

I also continue to be amazed at how few churches cooperate in min-istry to teenagers. There are more than enough young people to go around, yet tens of thousands of churches are protective and territorial about their outreach to youths. These days there are numerous ways of reaching kids—through on-campus events, the Internet, off-campus activities, community service projects, small groups, etc. If we were able to see our work as a Kingdom venture, rather than a congregational ven-ture whose boundaries must be carefully and closely protected, then even greater results might be achieved.

I have also been impressed by the fact that the most meaningful spir-itual growth that occurs these days is that which is customized to the needs of the individual. Rather than pat ourselves on the back for hav-ing large numbers of kids in the same place at the same time, all listen-ing to the same message, we ought to be saddened by the realization that we are losing most kids when we conduct a one-size-fits-all ministry. Because young people have divergent backgrounds, knowledge and needs, the most effective youth ministries in the nation customize what they offer to the specific needs of each kid. Time consuming? You bet.

Labor intensive? Absolutely. Worthwhile? Without question. Creating a spiritual development plan for each teenager, created in cooperation with them, and having them craft personal spiritual goals and an accountability process to which they agree can make all the difference between having a youth ministry that fills an auditorium and one that changes lives.

WHICH DO YOU WANT?

Let me also return to a theme I touched upon earlier in this book: the importance of getting teenagers to embrace absolute moral truths as conveyed to us by God in the Bible. Perhaps the single most important challenge facing youth workers today is to help young people understand and own absolute moral truth. Until we champion this issue, and help teens to master it, we are just throwing mud on the gaping holes in a dike.

Does this issue really matter that much? I believe it is the crux of America's demise, and represents the cornerstone of effective ministry—to anyone, youth or adult. We can claim that evangelism is the most important ministry thrust, but unless people understand that there are absolute moral truths to which the Christian faith is connected, then evangelism is likely to be like the seed sown in the rocky soil or amidst the weeds—rootless and ultimately overpowered by the world.

Consider this: If people do not accept the existence of absolute moral truth, then we will not get very far by describing to them the consequences of their sin. Why not? Because if there is no absolute moral truth, then there can be no difference between right and wrong. That then means there really is no such thing as sin, which implies that there cannot be judgment. Without judgment there is no condemnation, and without condemnation there is no need to be saved. Without a need for salvation, Jesus becomes a good teacher who performed some mighty works. But the eternal need for such a Savior is eliminated—simply because there is no absolute moral truth.

The problem persists even among believers. Take the challenge of discipleship. If there is no absolute moral truth—and most born-again Christians contend that there is not—then there is no ultimate authority. Without such an authority, there cannot be universally appropriate standards of conduct and belief. That, in turn, means there is no righteousness and, consequently, no reliable principles upon which we must base our lives. Without such requirements we have no need to change our thinking and behavioral patterns, which results in the absence of any compelling reason to study the Bible and integrate its teachings into our lives.

The same challenge exists regarding worship. In the absence of absolute moral truth there is no ultimate authority, which means that there is not an omnipotent, omniscient and loving—but holy—God who deserves our worship. Worship is thus converted into an exercise of demonstrating appreciation for good deeds, rather than a heartfelt expression of awe, humility and gratitude in response to the One who embodies truth.

We simply cannot overestimate the significance of the truth issue in our culture today. However, we often underestimate its importance in the practice of ministry, lifestyle choices and personal relationships.

How did our young people become so confused—or complacent—about truth? It stems from a variety of errant inputs. First, their role models have consistently denied the existence of such truth and have lived accordingly. Second, our culture upholds relativism and encourages people to be "open-minded" on all things. The mass media, public policy makers and even our schools have facilitated the acceptance of relativism. Third, the Church is guilty of not providing people with substance that clarifies truth. We teach about many topics and exegete many passages of Scripture, but rarely do congregants hear a cohesive argument for the existence and practical application of truth. It is even more rare to discover a church whose teaching is intentionally designed to continually enable people to grasp the content of moral truth, in the context of a comprehensive and coherent worldview. Fourth, people are ill-equipped to dissect Scripture on their own to get at the issues. Fifth, people's priorities do not include a deeper understanding of the core issues of life. Millions of Americans are concerned about increasing their salary or buying a new car or new home; few are actively wrestling with the deeper purpose of life and how the raise, the car or the house fit into a framework of ultimate meaning.

What are you doing—in your family, in your church, in your youth ministry—to enable young people to understand the notion of moral truth, the idea of absolutism in a culture of relativism, and to commit to developing a biblical worldview that is founded on God's unchanging and non-negotiable truths?[2]

THIS REALLY MATTERS!

Teenagers matter. Your ministry to teenagers—whether you are a senior pastor, a youth pastor, a youth worker, a teacher or a parent—matters. You are shaping the future of the nation. You are determining the future of the Church. You are affecting the character and souls of the emerging leaders of the world. What a challenge! What a privilege! If you like to be where the action is, and want to make a difference in the world, there may be no more strategic ministry for you to accept than to work with teenagers.

Cool . . .

Notes

1. For a more detailed discussion of the nature and practice of Socratic evangelism, see various sections of my earlier book *Evangelism That Works* (Ventura, CA: Regal Books, 1995).
2. I have written more extensively on this matter in *The Second Coming of the Church* (Nashville, TN: Word, 1998).

RESEARCH
METHODOLOGY

This report is based on data derived from five nationwide surveys among teenagers conducted by the Barna Research Group, Ltd. of Ventura, CA. In each survey a random sample of teenagers was drawn from the 48 continental states and a survey questionnaire was administered to individuals who were 13 to 18 years of age. The four telephone surveys were conducted from the Barna Research field facility in Ventura, and the mail survey was sent from the main office in Ventura to households that contained at least one teenager. The timing and related statistics pertaining to those five surveys are shown on the following page:

Survey	Data Collection	Dates Conducted	Sample Size	Margin of Error* Error*
YouthPoll 98	telephone	October 1998	605	±4 points
Peace Index	mail	March 1998	1028	±3 points
YouthPoll 99	telephone	November 1999	614	±4 points
YouthPoll 00A	telephone	July 2000	601	±4 points
YouthPoll 00B	telephone	September 2000	605	±4 points

Note: * based on the 95% confidence level. The "95% confidence level" means that we can be 95% certain that the statistics reported are truly representative of the aggregate population from which the sample was draw, within the sample error parameters (i.e., the "plus or minus x percentage points").

The YouthPoll surveys are annual tracking studies among teenagers, conducted by Barna Research to remain abreast of what is happening in the lives of people from 13 to 18 years of age in the United States. The Peace Index study was conducted in conjunction with KidsPeace, a non-profit organization located in Schnecksville, Pennsylvania, and dedicated to helping adolescents and teenagers. KidsPeace phone number is 1-800-257-3223. Permission to use the results of the survey was granted by KidsPeace.

The surveys were conducted through the use of random digit-dial sampling technique. In this method we derive a representative nationwide sample of telephone numbers that have been randomly generated. We then call the household and screen respondents to determine whether or not a teen lives in the home. If so, we attempt to conduct the interview with the teen. While we are not able to connect with every eligible teenager, our response rates in qualified households exceed industry norms. In these surveys, the response rates averaged 78 percent in the qualified households. The average survey lasted 18 minutes per respondent.

Lastly, for those not familiar with statistics, it is important to note two points that might otherwise be a cause of confusion for the reader:

- "N"="base size"="sample size"
- Whenever responses add up to less than 100% in any given category, it is either because we did not include the "don't know" responses or because those percentages shown have been rounded off.

ABOUT THE AUTHOR

George Barna is the president of the Barna Research Group, Ltd., a marketing research firm located in Ventura, CA. The company specializes in conducting primary research for Christian ministries and nonprofit organizations. Since its inception in 1984, Barna Research has served several hundred parachurch ministries and thousands of Christian churches. The firm has also helped a number of for-profit clients in the media, communications and political arenas.

To date, Barna has written 30 books. Among his most recent releases are *Growing True Disciples*, *Building Effective Lay Leadership Teams*, *Re-Churching the Unchurched* and *Boiling Point*. He is also the author of several best-sellers such as *The Frog in the Kettle*, *The Second Coming of the Church*, *User-Friendly Churches*, *Marketing the Church* and *The Power of Vision*. Several of his books have received national awards. He has also written for numerous periodicals and has published more than two dozen syndicated reports on a variety of topics related to ministry. His work is frequently cited as an authoritative source by the media.

Many people know Barna from his intensive seminars for church leaders that are produced by Barna Research and based on original research. He is a popular speaker at ministry conferences around the world and has taught at several universities and seminaries. He has served as a pastor of a large, multicultural church and has been involved in several church plants.

He has served on the board of directors and advisory board of various ministries, including Compassion International, Evangelicals for Social Action, the Mapping Center for Evangelism, International Students Inc., the Steve Russo Evangelistic Team and the Wagner Institute for Practical Leadership. He is the founding director of The Barna Institute, a nonprofit organization dedicated to providing strategic information to ministries.

After graduating summa cum laude from Boston College, Barna earned two masters degrees from Rutgers University and received a doctorate from Dallas Baptist University.

He lives with his wife, Nancy, and their two daughters, Samantha and Corban, in southern California. He enjoys spending time with his family, writing, reading, playing basketball or guitar, relaxing on the beach, visiting bookstores and eating pizza.

ABOUT THE BARNA RESEARCH GROUP

The Barna Research Group (BRG) was initiated in 1984 by George and Nancy Barna to serve the information needs of the Church. BRG's vision is "to provide Christian ministries with current, accurate and reliable information, in bite-sized pieces, at reasonable cost, to help them to be more strategic in their decision making." The company has been honored to serve thousands of ministries since its inception.

Here is how Barna Research helps ministries:

- offers a wealth of information online, through the BRG website www.brg.org

- conducts primary research related to specific information, development and marketing needs of an organization
- provides resources—books, reports, videos, audiocassettes, newsletters—that describe BRG's research and how the findings apply to ministry
- conducts intensive seminars for church leaders, revealing insights from primary research conducted for the seminar
- presents information in conferences, seminars and other meetings
- provides research-based consultation related to articulated ministry needs

BRG uses both quantitative and qualitative research methods to generate relevant and reliable information that reveals insights to enhance ministry efforts. Among the types of research commonly conducted by BRG are

- attitudinal and behavioral surveys of congregations;
- lifestyle, values, behavior and beliefs profiles of communities;
- profiles of the attitudes, expectations, giving habits and needs of donors;
- evaluations of new products: perceived value, pricing, marketing, etc.;
- name-recognition and ministry-image studies;
- employee-perception studies;
- efficiency and effectiveness studies;
- product-use studies;
- customer service and customer satisfaction;
- segmentation studies to identify tapped and untapped potential;
- media-use surveys.

If you would like to know more about Barna Research, please explore our website at www.barna.org. If you are interested in conducting primary research to solve some of your ministry and marketing challenges, call us at 1-800-55-BARNA.

TAKING ADVANTAGE
OF BARNA RESEARCH

Because our commitment is to help the Church live up to its God-given calling, we try to support ministries with strategic information. While much of the data and related interpretation are contained in the books and reports that we develop, we have created a website that is geared to arming ministers—lay and professional—with the strategic intelligence they need to make great decisions in ministry. Here are suggestions on how to take advantage of what we have to offer.

Visit our website at www.barna.org. Take some time to explore the various pages on the site to discover what we have to offer. You may not need it all today. But it might be useful in the future.

Subscribe to our free newsletter, The Barna Update, which is available only through the website. Every two weeks or so George Barna releases a new report based upon the most recent information from Barna Research surveys. Once you sign up you will automatically receive a very brief e-mail on the day the study is released to inform you of the topic of the report and two or three key findings. If the topic interests you, click on the link provided with the e-mail (or independently go to our website) to read the entire release. We have also included a function that enables you to click and send—that is, to send the report to others whom you feel would benefit from it. (By the way, after you do subscribe we will never give out your e-mail address or any other information about you. And we will not be spamming you from now until eternity!)

Use the data archives. We have put hundreds of factoids and data morsels into 40 different data categories that you can access. Need facts for a sermon? Ideas on how to make a Scripture passage more relevant? Want to understand what people are thinking and doing in relation to a specific topic? Interested in understanding more about different segments of the population? Use this 24/7 library of faith facts whenever you're seeking a particular insight.

Acquire related resources. If you are interested in additional information on specific topics, check out the reports, books, diagnostics, videos, audiocassettes and other resources based on our research that are available to you. Some of these resources can be obtained only through our website.

We are constantly updating and expanding our website content. We pray that you use it and profit from it. Let us know what else you want on the site. It's there for you.

www.barna.org